SECRETS OF THE MUMMIES

FIRST EDITION
Project Editors Mary Atkinson and Penny Smith; **Art Editor** Karen Lieberman;
Senior Editor Linda Esposito; **US Editor** Regina Kahney; **Pre-Production** Francesca Wardell;
Picture Researchers Andy Sampson and Kathy Lockley; **Illustrator** Peter Dennis;
Reading Consultant Linda Gambrell, PhD

THIS EDITION
Produced for DK by WonderLab Group LLC
Jennifer Emmett, Erica Green, Kate Hale, *Founders*
www.wonderlabgroup.com

Editors Grace Hill Smith, Libby Romero, Michaela Weglinski;
Photography Editors Kelley Miller, Annette Kiesow, Nicole DiMelle; **Managing Editor** Rachel Houghton;
Product Manager Sarah Forbes; **Design Director** Phil Ormerond; **Production** Andrew Beehag;
Designers Project Design Company; **Jacket Style Designer** Lisa Lanzarini; **Researcher** Michelle Harris;
Copy Editor Lori Merritt; **Indexer** Connie Binder; **Proofreader** Larry Shea; **Production** Andrew Beehag;
Reading Specialist Dr. Jennifer Albro; **Curriculum Specialist** Elaine Larson

Published in the United States by DK Publishing
1745 Broadway, 20th Floor, New York, NY 10019

Copyright © 2023 Dorling Kindersley Limited
DK, a Division of Penguin Random House LLC
24 25 26 27 28 10 9 8 7 6 5 4 3 2 1
001–341826–Mar/2024

A catalog record for this book
is available from the Library of Congress.
ISBN: 978-0-5938-4256-0

DK books are available at special discounts when purchased in bulk for sales promotions, premiums,
fundraising, or educational use. For details, contact: DK Publishing Special Markets,
1745 Broadway, 20th Floor, New York, NY 10019
SpecialSales@dk.com

Printed and bound in China

The publisher would like to thank the following for their kind permission to reproduce their images:
a=above; c=center; b=below; l=left; r=right; t=top; b/g=background

Alamy Stock Photo: dpa picture alliance / Sebastian Kahnert 45clb; **Dreamstime.com:** Andrey Donnikov 26tl, Sl Photography 29b;
Getty Images: AFP / Bruno Ferrandez 45tr, Hulton Archive 16tl, 21b, Hulton Fine Art Collection / Art Images 22tr

Cover images: *Front:* **Dreamstime.com:** Jaroslav Moravcik b; **Getty Images:** Mint Images; *Back:* **Shutterstock.com:** Little.Kalu cla,
Macrovector cra, cl

All other images © Dorling Kindersley
For more information see: www.dkimages.com

www.dk.com

This book was made with Forest
Stewardship Council™ certified
paper - one small step in DK's
commitment to a sustainable future.
**For more information go to
www.dk.com/our-green-pledge**

SECRETS
OF THE
MUMMIES

Harriet Griffey

CONTENTS

6 People from the Past

8 Making a Mummy

16 The Mummy's Curse

24 Inca Emperor Mummies

30 Inca Ice Maiden

34 Sicilian Mummies

40 The Mummy Mystery

44 Mummies Today

46 Glossary

47 Index

48 Quiz

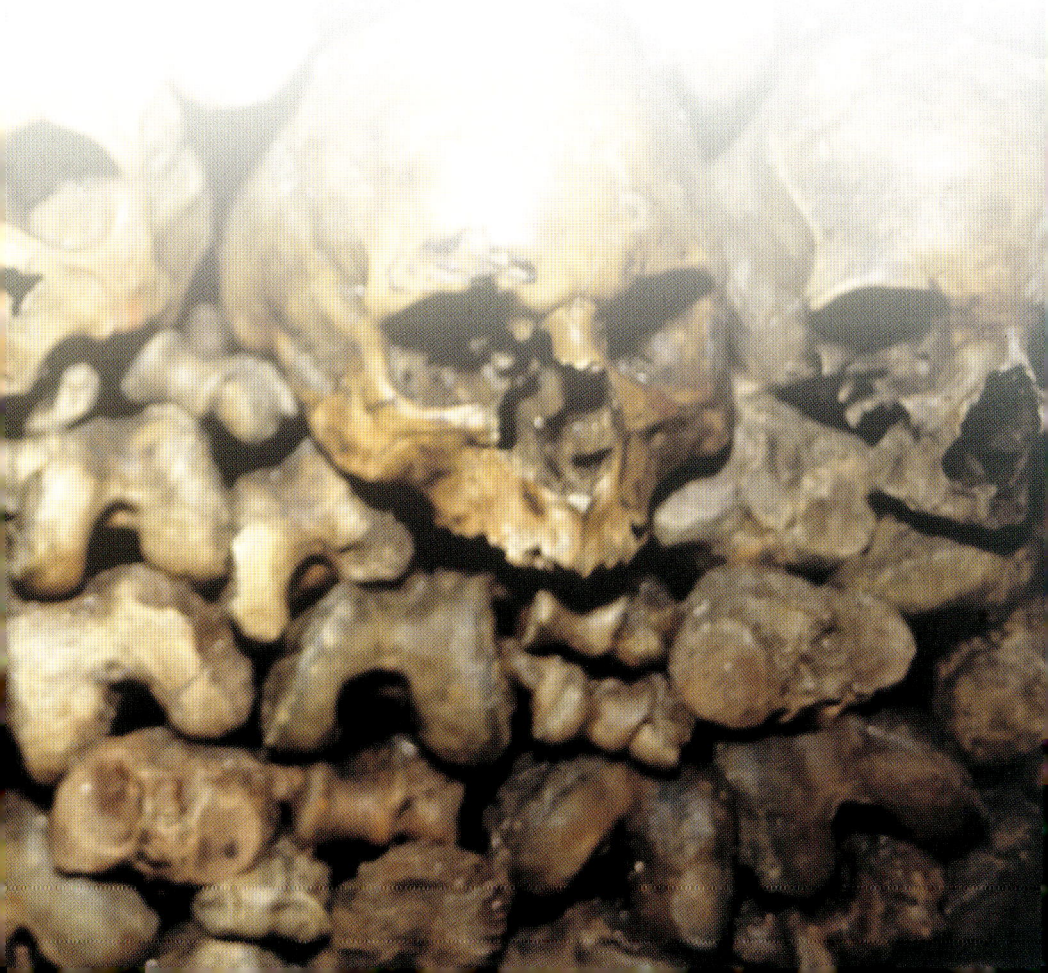

Teenage Boy
Some Roman mummies were decorated with a realistic painting of the person who had died.

Animals
The ancient Egyptians believed cats were sacred. They often mummified cats' bodies when they died.

PEOPLE FROM THE PAST

There is something intriguing about a mummy. It is hard to believe that hundreds or even thousands of years ago it was a living person.

A mummy is the preserved body of someone who has died. The body may have been preserved naturally or deliberately as part of a religious ritual.

Naturally preserved bodies have been discovered in airless bogs. Here, the animals and bacteria that usually break down bodies cannot survive, so the body does not decay. This can also happen in hot, dry deserts and on icy mountains.

This mummy was found in a Danish bog. It is the body of a man who died more than 1,500 years ago.

Other bodies were carefully preserved by people. The most famous mummies belong to the ancient Egyptians. But other cultures, such as the Incas of South America and the Pazyryks of Siberia, also used to preserve their dead. Some people buried their mummies with artifacts, such as bowls, statues, and beautiful jewels.

This book investigates different mummies discovered around the world. We'll look first at how the ancient Egyptians made a mummy.

Artifacts
Everyday objects were often buried with mummies.

Important Doll
Figures, such as this Peruvian doll, were buried with a mummy to bring the dead person luck in the afterlife.

Statue of an Egyptian priest

MAKING A MUMMY

For 3,000 years, the ancient Egyptian civilization flourished. The people living then had strong beliefs about gods and life after death. They thought that if a dead person's spirit could recognize its preserved body, it would live forever in the afterlife.

Wealthy Egyptians paid the chief priests to mummify the bodies of their loved ones. They believed that the priests could help decide a person's fate after death.

Immediately after someone died, a chief priest would send a servant to summon other priests. They would be needed to help embalm the body—a process that stops the body from decaying.

Then, the chief priest would gather his tools and set off for his workshop on the west bank of the Nile River.

Meanwhile, other servants collected the body and carried it to the workshop. There they laid it on a special table, ready for the ceremony to begin.

The chief priest put on a jackal-headed mask to represent Anubis, the Egyptian god of mummification. Then, he slowly washed the body while another priest read magic spells out loud. When the body was clean enough, the embalming process began.

This ancient Egyptian painting shows a body being washed.

After being washed, the body was left to dry.

Tools
These tools were used in a ritual intended to enable the mummy to eat and drink in the afterlife.

Jackal Mask
At embalming ceremonies, jackal–headed masks, such as this pottery one, represented Anubis, god of mummification.

Incision
A cut was usually made down the left side of the body.

Embalming knife
This ceremonial knife has a sharp blade made of flint.

The chief priest picked up an embalming knife and carefully made a long cut down the left side of the body. Then he put his hand into the cut and pulled out the liver, lungs, stomach, and guts. Each of these was stored in a canopic jar—a special container in the shape of a god.

The next part was difficult. He had to push a thin bronze hook up the dead person's nose and, bit by bit, scoop out the brain.

Hapy (HAH-pee) was a baboon god who guarded the lungs.

The falcon god Qebehsenuef (keb-ekh-SEN-oo-ef) guarded the intestines, or guts.

The brain was thrown away because the ancient Egyptians did not understand what it was for, so they did not think it was important.

After this, the body was ready to be dried. The priests heaped natron, a natural salt, over the body to draw out all the fluids. It would take 40 days for the body to dry completely.

Only then would the body be ready for the next step.

Natron
This natural salt is found by the edges of desert lakes.

Magical Figures
These figures lay on the body to guard the places where the organs had been removed.

Son of Horus
The four gods who guarded canopic jars were the sons of Horus, god of the sky.

Imsety (im-SET-ee) was a human-like god who guarded the liver.

The jackal-headed god Duamutef (do-ah-MOO-tef) guarded the stomach.

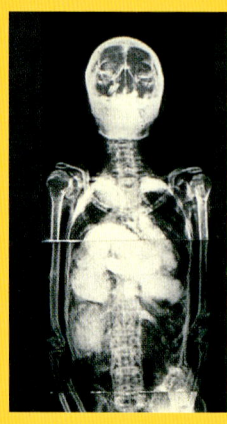

Stuffing
This x-ray of a mummy shows linen stuffing replacing some of the organs.

Scarab beetle

Wadjet eye

Amulets
These were good luck charms. The wadjet eye was believed to keep away evil.

After 40 days, the dried body was filled with linen, sand, or sawdust to help it keep its shape. Beeswax was pushed into the nostrils, and linen was stuffed into the eye sockets. Next, oils and spices were rubbed into the skin to keep it from cracking.

Now the chief priest was ready to begin wrapping the body. He wound thin linen strips around each finger. Then, he bandaged the arms and legs and the rest of the body.

Magical figures called amulets were wrapped in between the layers of cloth. At the same time, the priest brushed the bandages with resin to stick them together. Bandaging the body could take 15 days.

Finally, the mummified body was placed in a coffin. If everything had gone well, the chief priest was pleased. All the dead person needed now was some magic spells.

Nest of Coffins
Sometimes, the coffin was put into a bigger coffin, which might then be put into an even bigger coffin, and so on.

Scribes
In ancient Egypt, only scribes could write. They were highly respected people.

A scribe, or writer, handed the priests a scroll. The scroll was the *Book of the Dead*—a special book containing more than 200 spells. It was placed inside the coffin.

The ancient Egyptians believed that the dead person would need to recite the spells in the book to gain protection on his or her journey to the Hall of the Two Truths.

Scary Figures
Figures like this hippo were put in the tomb to scare off intruders.

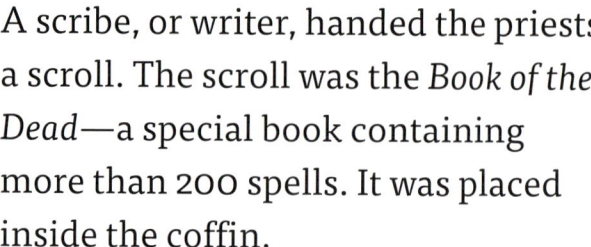

Hapy, the baboon god

The "Devourer of the Dead" waiting to eat the hearts of evil people

Anubis, god of mummification

Feather of truth

Heart of the dead person

In this judgment hall, the great god Osiris was believed to watch over a ceremony where the dead person had to deny all his or her bad deeds.

Anubis, the jackal-headed god, used scales to balance the person's heart against the "feather of truth." If the heart was not too heavy with bad deeds, the dead person was allowed to live in the afterlife.

Back in this world, the dead person's family filled a tomb with food and treasures for the mummy to use in the afterlife. Curses were often written over the coffin and the walls of the tomb, warning intruders of terrible punishments for stealing.

But over the centuries, grave robbers broke into the tombs looking for treasure. A legend grew that somewhere in the Egyptian Valley of the Kings lay a rich, untouched tomb—the tomb of the young pharaoh Tutankhamun.

Underworld
It was thought that everyone passed through this land on their way to the afterlife. They began their journey by crossing the Nile River.

God of Death
Osiris was king of the afterworld, which was thought to be like Egypt but better.

THE MUMMY'S CURSE

"I must find the lost tomb."

Howard Carter had been saying the same thing for years. Now it was 1922, the fifth year he had spent digging through sand and rocks in Egypt's Valley of the Kings. He was searching for a tomb that no grave robbers had ever found—the tomb of Tutankhamun, the boy pharaoh.

Carter scoffed when he was warned of the curse: "Death comes on wings to he who enters the tomb of a pharaoh."

Howard Carter
After traveling to Egypt as a young artist, Carter's interest turned to investigating ancient Egypt.

Pharaoh
The pharaohs were the kings of ancient Egypt. They were believed to be living gods.

Each day, his team worked in the sweltering heat and dust. They seemed to be getting nowhere. Then, one morning, as they dug in soft rubble, a shovel clanged.

When Carter arrived, he was met by an excited hush. The team had found a stone step. Another 15 steps were quickly uncovered. Could this be Tutankhamun's tomb?

Tutankhamun
This pharaoh ruled from around 1361 BCE to 1352 BCE. He was 19 years old when he died.

Valley of the Kings
To avoid grave robbers, many pharaohs chose this remote place for their tombs.

17

Carnarvon
This wealthy English lord visited Egypt for his health. His interest in tombs began as a way to pass the time.

Hieroglyphs
Each symbol in this ancient Egyptian writing stands for a word or a sound.

The staircase led to a sealed door. Carter wanted to open it, but he had to wait. Lord Carnarvon, his patron, had paid for the years of work and wanted to be present at the opening.

Today, it would take only six hours to reach Egypt from Carnarvon's home in England, but at that time, it took more than two weeks. When Carnarvon finally arrived, he hurried to the tomb. Nervously, he fingered the strange symbols, called hieroglyphs, by the door. Then, he and Carter opened the door and crept inside.

The two men pushed their way through a rock-filled corridor, which led to another sealed door. Cautiously, they made a hole in the door.

Carter was the first to look. What he saw left him speechless. Later, he told people that he had seen "strange animals, statues, and gold—everywhere the glint of gold."

The room was untidily packed with priceless treasures. There were sparkling gems, animal-shaped beds, beautiful painted boxes, and a magnificent golden throne.

Nothing had been touched for 3,000 years!

Wide-eyed, the pair picked their way through the riches. Then, they came to a third sealed doorway. They were desperate to know where it led, but again they had to wait. First, all these things had to be carefully sorted.

The paintings on this treasure chest show Tutankhamun conquering his enemies.

Tomb Jewels
This vulture represented the goddess Nekhabet, and this scarab beetle ornament represented the sun god Khepri.

Afterlife of Luxury
The ancient Egyptians filled the king's tomb with treasure, such as golden sandals and precious jewels, for him to use in the afterlife.

Kingly Killer
While the cobra can kill people if disturbed, it also helps rid towns of rats and mice.

Royal Dummy
Statues of Tutankhamun often show a cobra on his headdress. This wooden statue is a dummy found in the tomb.

When Carter arrived home that night, his servants were wailing and shouting.

"What's wrong?" Carter demanded above the din.

"You have opened the tomb," wept a servant. "We are cursed!" He told Carter that a cobra had swallowed Carter's pet canary at the exact moment the tomb was opened. Cobras were a symbol of royalty in ancient Egypt. They were said to spit fire at a pharaoh's enemies.

Carter was not worried. The next day, he began to clear the first room of the tomb.

More than a mile of cotton wadding was used to wrap up the items. Carter's team packed games, clothing, pottery, musical instruments, and statues. Most of these were sent to Cairo, Egypt's capital, by boat. The more valuable artifacts went on a train accompanied by armed guards.

Finally, they were ready to unseal the third door. Slowly and carefully, Carter started chipping away the rocks and plaster. Then, he stopped. Before him was a wall of solid gold! It was the front of a huge, golden shrine. Carter was astonished. He knew this was the greatest ancient Egyptian find ever.

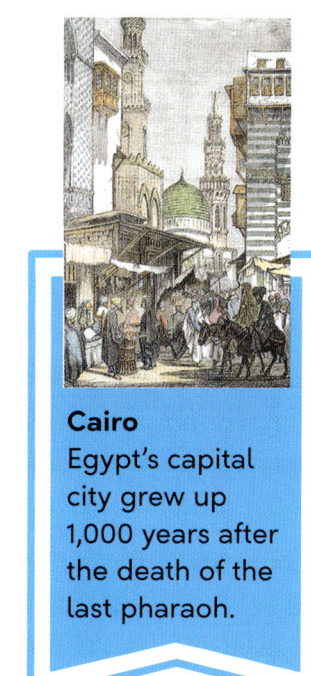

Cairo
Egypt's capital city grew up 1,000 years after the death of the last pharaoh.

Howard Carter (left) and his assistants carefully wrap a life-size statue.

Kingly Coffin
The middle coffin was made of wood covered in gold with inlaid glass.

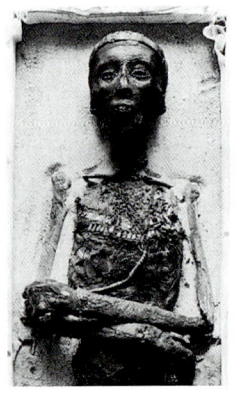

Royal Mummy
Although the riches in the tomb were in good condition, Tutankhamun's mummy was badly decayed.

Inside the golden shrine were three more shrines. And inside the last one was a sarcophagus—a stone coffin. But that was not all. Within the sarcophagus were three more coffins, each fitting snugly inside the other. The final coffin was made of solid gold. Inside it was the mummified body of Tutankhamun.

But before anyone could investigate further, disaster struck. It began when Carter's patron, Lord Carnarvon, was bitten on the cheek by a mosquito.

He accidentally cut open the bite while shaving. The bite soon became infected, and fever set in.

A few days later, Carnarvon's family raced to his bedside. He was very ill. Then, early one morning, it was all over. Lord Carnarvon died.

At the very moment of his death, all the lights in Cairo went out. They stayed out for several hours, and no one could explain why. Back at Lord Carnarvon's home in England, Susie, his dog, pricked up her ears, howled once, then dropped dead.

Other deaths followed. A French scientist who visited the tomb died after a fall. An x-ray specialist on his way to examine Tutankhamun's mummy died unexpectedly. Then, an American died from a virus after visiting the tomb. Were these deaths all coincidences, or was the curse of the mummy to blame? No one knows for sure.

Despite the threat of a curse, many objects have been removed from Egyptian tombs over time. It is now illegal to take these items out of the country. Egyptian authorities have retrieved many items as they work to restore their country's heritage.

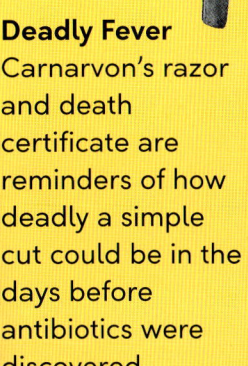

Deadly Fever
Carnarvon's razor and death certificate are reminders of how deadly a simple cut could be in the days before antibiotics were discovered.

A Royal Match
In 1902, Carter found the tomb of Queen Hatshepsut, a famous female pharaoh who ruled Egypt in the 15th century BCE. In 2006, a team of researchers returned to the site. They found a tooth in a box that bore the queen's name. The tooth matched a gap in the jaw of a mummy lying in the tomb.

Inca Empire
This empire covered parts of what are now Colombia, Ecuador, Peru, Bolivia, Chile, and Argentina.

Sun Temples
Many temples were built in honor of Inti, god of the sun.

INCA EMPEROR MUMMIES

As dawn broke, drumbeats sounded through the city of Cuzco (KOOZ-koe). The people began to wake, and an excited buzz filled the air. It was the most important day of the year in the Inca Empire, a civilization that covered much of South America 500 years ago.

Today was Inti Raimi (IN-tee RYE-me), a religious festival held in honor of Inti, the sun god. Every year, this festival was celebrated on June 21, midwinter's day. By showing thanks and honoring Inti, the Inca people believed that summer would come once more and their crops would grow.

Temples were built from carefully shaped blocks of stone. Sun temples were often filled with solid gold models of cornstalks, lumps of earth, and other things related to farming.

Everyone in the Inca Empire gave one-third of all they produced to the priests of the sun god. Many of these plants and animals were sacrificed in special ceremonies held throughout the year. Today's ceremonies were the most important of all.

Inca Year
The Incas had a religious festival for each month. Inti Raimi was held in June, which is the coldest month of the year in South America.

Priests began to chant in time with the drumbeats. In the Holy Square, a large crowd gathered. The people were excited but quiet and respectful. They were waiting for the Procession of the Living Dead.

Sun Disc
The sun god was represented in many Inca temples by gold discs with human faces.

Llamas
The llama is related to the camel. Llamas are still used in South America for wool, meat, and transportation.

At last, the crowds spotted the white llamas that always led the procession. There were hundreds of llamas walking in lines, one after another.

Behind the llamas came a litter carrying the emperor, the Sapa Inca. Everyone in the crowd knelt down, hid their faces in their hands, and prayed. Ordinary people were not allowed to look at the Sapa Inca.

Next came litters, or stretchers, bearing the mummified bodies of the long-dead former Sapa Incas.

Each mummy was worshipped as a son of the sun god. It was thought that the living Sapa Inca received advice and help from these mummies.

Sometimes, a child would sneak a look. He or she would glimpse the mummies, each draped in beautiful cloth woven from the soft wool of the vicuna, a relative of the llama.

But even a peeking child would not see the emperors' faces. They were covered with golden masks, which the priests believed would protect the emperors in the afterlife.

Litters
These beds, or stretchers, were used to carry the mummies in processions.

Huari Mummy
The Huari people lived near Cuzco before the Incas. They too mummified their leaders.

Gods
Incas had great respect for their gods. They gave them offerings, such as statues, gold, animals, and sometimes even people.

Chica
This alcoholic drink was made from corn. It was stored in decorated clay jars.

The procession stopped at the Temple of the Sun, where more ceremonies began. It was a long day, full of prayer. The people thought that if they pleased the mummified Sapa Incas, they would please the sun god.

In the evening, things became a little more festive. The city's inhabitants feasted on roasted llamas served with corn cakes and potatoes. The adults drank freshly brewed chica, an alcoholic drink. There was singing and dancing until late at night. But even during the feast, the sun god was not forgotten. The very best food was put in front of the god's sons, the mummified emperors.

At the end of the day, the mummies were returned to the palaces where they had lived when they were alive. These palaces were still kept in order by specially chosen workers.

The workers fanned the air to keep flies off the mummies. They offered the mummies food and water when they felt it was needed. Most importantly, they delivered messages to the mummies and interpreted their replies.

The people believed that long-gone ancestors could give advice. It did not matter that these emperors were dead—they were still considered very powerful.

Mummified Bodies
For more than 4,000 years, people across South America mummified their dead.

After the Spaniards conquered the Incas in 1532, they built a church on the site of the old Temple of the Sun in Cuzco.

The Andes
This is the longest chain of mountains in the world. The Andes' snowcapped peaks run through Peru and Chile.

Look-Alike
The goddess statue was made of gold and dressed in clothes similar to the girl's.

INCA ICE MAIDEN

The climbers were weary. It had taken three days to reach the top of Nevado Ampato, a high mountain in the Peruvian Andes. The paths were steep and the air was thin, making it difficult to breathe. But finally the four priests reached their destination—the top of the icy ridge.

From packs tied to the llamas, they unloaded pots, food, figurines, and a small statue of a goddess. Then, they set up a small stone altar.

With the group of priests was a 13-year-old girl, the daughter of an important Inca family. Under a warm blanket, she wore a beautiful belted dress of rich yellow, purple, and red wool.

One of the priests led the girl to the altar. She took off the blankets, and the priest draped a finely woven cloth over her shoulders. He fastened the cloth with a silver pin.

Finally, while chanting special prayers, the chief priest placed a large feathered headdress on the girl's head.

Headdress
The girl's headdress was made of macaw feathers. These bird feathers were often used in religious ceremonies.

31

Last Resort
The Incas stored food in case of a famine. But if there was a long famine, the people appealed to the gods.

Llama Herd
Statues were often used in ceremonies. This llama statue may have reminded the gods to provide grass for their herds to eat.

The unusual group had traveled to the mountain because of a severe three-year drought, or water shortage. Crops had failed, and the people were starving. The priests believed that the drought occurred because the gods were angry.

After much prayer and talk, they had decided that a special sacrifice should be made to the mountain god—they must sacrifice someone who was almost perfect. That person would live forever with the gods in the afterlife. Such a sacrifice would surely please the gods and bring rain.

The girl and her family were a little frightened when she was chosen, but they also felt very honored.

Now the girl sat by a fire as the priests dug a large hole in the frozen ground. They lined the hole with sacred red earth, then placed cups, pots, and food in it for the girl to use in the afterlife.

The priests' chanting grew louder. It was time. The chief priest bent down to hand the girl a strong drink. After a few sips, she slipped into unconsciousness and died. Her body was gently wrapped in thick cloth and laid in the tomb.

When a volcano erupted 500 years later, ash fell on Nevado Ampato, melting the ice. In September 1995, scientists studying the damage found the girl's body. It had been mummified by the freezing cold. Her face had decayed, but the rest of her body was still in almost perfect condition.

Mountain Discovery
The two men who discovered the girl's body carried it down the mountain as fast as they could so it would not thaw and decay. It is now stored in a freezer at a university in Peru, where it is studied and preserved.

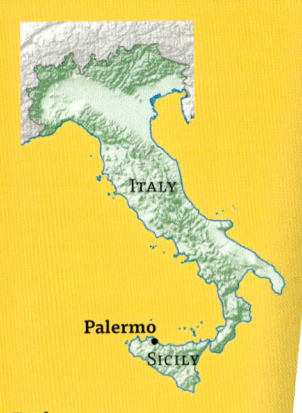

SICILIAN MUMMIES

In the Sicilian city of Palermo, an unusual, centuries-old tradition continued right up until the 1920s.

Deep below a Catholic church was an underground cemetery, called a catacomb. It housed the mummified bodies of 6,000 people! Instead of being horrified, locals would often visit the catacomb. In the cool, dark corridors, a child would be unafraid to raise a creaking coffin lid. Inside could be the body of the child's own great-grandmother!

Palermo
This is the largest city on the Italian island of Sicily.

Picnics
Families often made visits to the cemetery and would take a picnic lunch!

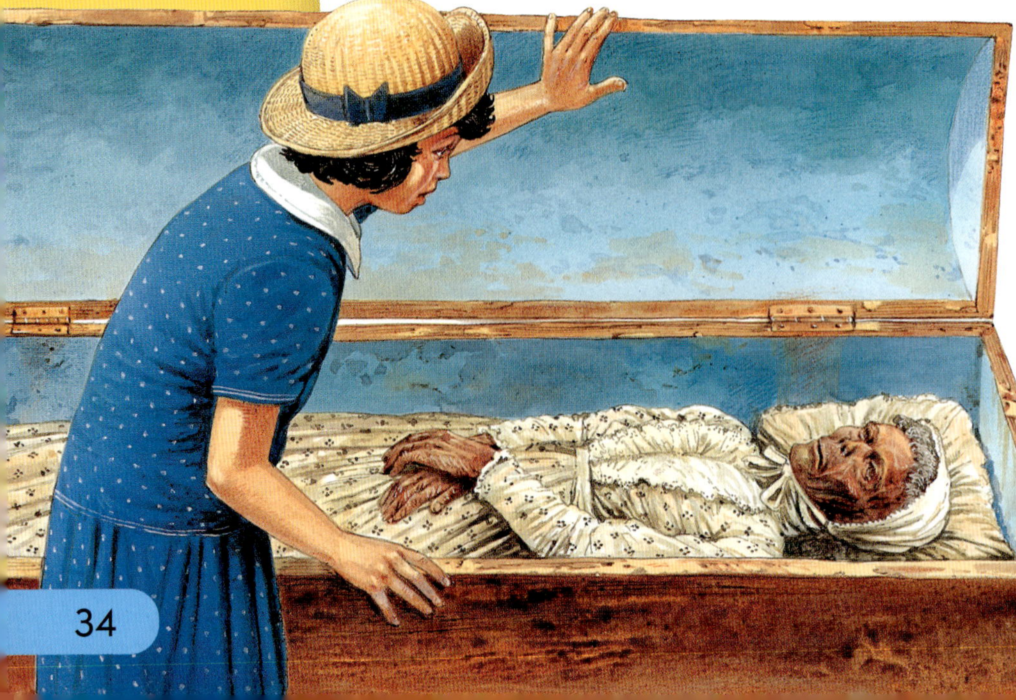

Many of the mummies
lie on benches. Labels
tell visitors who they are.

Tourist Attraction
Today, the mummies of Sicily attract thousands of visitors from all over the world.

Monk
Palermo's first mummies were the bodies of highly respected monks.

The people went to pay their respects to the mummies, to tell them stories, and to ask their advice. They did not find the mummies upsetting because their families had been visiting the cemetery for more than 300 years. It was simply part of ordinary life. They believed the mummies were a link with loved and respected relatives who had died.

Occasionally, the visitors would see a hooded figure moving silently among the coffins.

Again they were unafraid. They knew it was just one of the monks who looked after the catacomb.

These bearded and robed priests lived in a monastery next to the church. Since 1599, they had been mummifying the bodies of respected monks. Other people soon discovered what was happening and began asking for their relatives' bodies to be mummified in return for a donation to the church. They dressed the dead person in his or her best clothes before taking the body to the monastery.

Monks
The monks who look after the catacomb today still wear the brown robes they have worn for hundreds of years.

Clothing
The mummies provide us with information about the styles of clothes people wore in the past.

Father da Grubbio
This monk died in 1599. The monks today give him a gentle dusting with a vacuum cleaner each year.

The mummification process took over a year to complete—but how it was done was kept secret for hundreds of years!

Some of the mummies are quite gruesome to look at. The mummy of Father Silvestro da Grubbio, the oldest mummy of all, has four laughing skulls displayed around it. When Father da Grubbio died, his body was taken to a special cellar, where it lay over clay pipes for a whole year. This allowed all the body fluids to drain away.

These pipes were used to drain the bodies.

After that, the monks laid the body in the hot Sicilian sun to dry out. Then, they washed it in vinegar and, last of all, wrapped it in straw and sweet-smelling herbs. In spite of this, Father da Grubbio's mummy now looks more like a dressed skeleton.

As time went by, the monks improved their embalming process. Their new methods included soaking the body in arsenic or milk of magnesia. This left the skin far softer and gave it a more lifelike color.

The monks stopped mummifying bodies in 1920, but the mummies are still there. Today, the monks take tourists around the catacomb.

Soft Skin
The mummies made in the 1800s still have their skin and hair today.

Juan Perón
Perón was elected president of Argentina in 1946.

Buenos Aires
Evita was 15 years old when she went to live alone in Argentina's capital city.

THE MUMMY MYSTERY

On July 26, 1952, Pedro Ara's phone rang. "Come quickly," said the caller, "Evita is dying. President Perón is asking for you."

After a year's illness, Evita, the Argentinian president's wife, was dying of cancer.

During her life, Evita had won the hearts of the people. She had set up hospitals and helped the poor. She had also made sure that women in Argentina were allowed to vote.

The president wanted to make sure the people never forgot his wife. He hired Ara, a doctor and expert embalmer, to preserve her body. The president planned to erect a building, called Monument to the People, where Evita would rest.

At 8:25 pm, Evita died. Ara immediately began his secret work. Slowly and carefully, he replaced Evita's blood with glycerol, a thick liquid that would not decay. Then, he placed chemicals in her coffin to kill any insects or bacteria that might attack the body.

Evita's body was then dressed in a white gown and placed in a glass-topped coffin. For 16 days, more than 2,000,000 visitors filed past the coffin on display, many weeping and bending to kiss the glass lid.

But Ara began to worry. The glass case was opened twice to wipe away mist on the inside. It was not good for air to get to the body.

Evita
Evita was born Maria Eva Duarte, the youngest child in a poor family. She later became a popular actress and met many important people, including Juan Perón.

Evita was a passionate speaker loved by many Argentinians.

Sleeping Beauty
Many people who visited Evita's coffin dressed in black or wore their best clothes as a sign of respect.

Resting Place
Evita's body now rests in Recoleta Cemetery in Buenos Aires. It is said to lie in a bombproof compartment.

The coffin was taken to Ara's laboratory. There the body was repeatedly soaked in a bath of chemicals and injected with more preservatives. Finally, it was covered in a thin layer of clear plastic. It took Ara a year to complete the work, but he knew that the body would last forever.

Meanwhile, life in Argentina had become unsettled. President Perón had been overthrown by the army and forced to leave the country.

The new ruler, President Pedro Aramburu, did not want anything around that might encourage Perón's supporters. He canceled the plans for the Monument to the People and looked for somewhere else to place Evita's body.

Colonel Carlos Koenig, head of Army Intelligence, offered help. Shortly afterward, in November 1955, the body disappeared. Many stories began to circulate around Argentina about where it had gone.

After Aramburu's death in 1970, his lawyer handed over an envelope that solved the mystery.

In September 1971, gravediggers at an Italian cemetery were told to open the tomb of a woman called Maria Maggi de Magistris.

Inside the tomb was a perfectly preserved body. But it was not Maria Maggi. It was Evita Perón! The body had been secretly buried there 14 years earlier.

In 1974, Evita's body was returned to Argentina. She was laid to rest in her family tomb.

A Grieving Nation
People had to wait hours to see Evita's body. The huge crowds stretched for 3 miles (5 km).

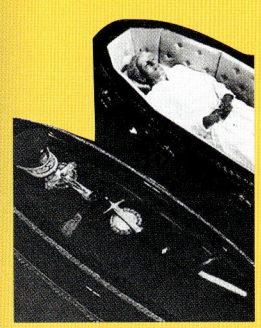

Together Again
In 1974, when Juan Perón died, he was not embalmed. His closed coffin was displayed next to Evita's open one.

Evita at rest in her coffin

MUMMIES TODAY

Today's fascination with mummies began when the French general Napoleon Bonaparte invaded Egypt in 1798. Teams of French scholars began to study the ancient Egyptian civilization.

But much of the evidence had already been destroyed. Thousands of mummies had been burned as fuel, ground up for medicine, or simply left to decay.

The first mummies transported to the West were treated little better. Many were "unwrapped" during exhibitions, destroying vital information in the process.

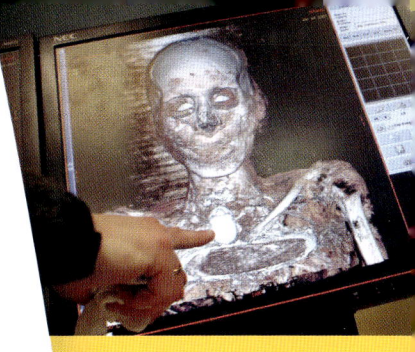

Scientists use mummies to find out what diseases people suffered from in the past. They use microscopes to look at skin, bone, and other body tissues.

Advances in technology have allowed people to take better care of ancient finds. In 1895, x-rays were discovered. An x-ray picture shows scientists what is inside a mummy case. Mummies no longer need to be unwrapped to be studied.

An Inside Look
This x-ray of an Inca mummy shows that the brain has shrunk to a small round ball at the base of the skull.

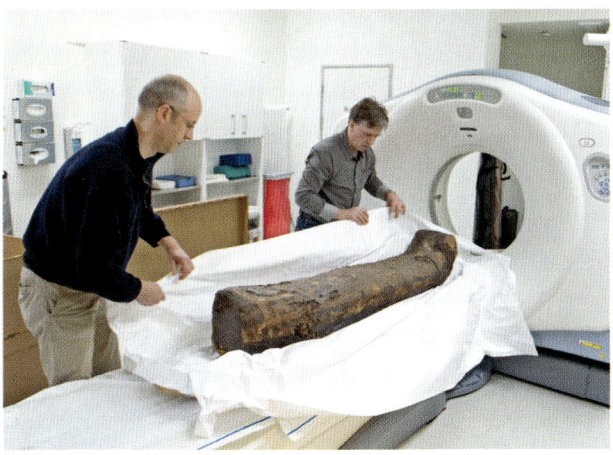

A mummy about to enter a CT scanner

A Peek Inside
A CT scan can show the skin on a mummy's face. At another setting, the machine could show the bone below the skin.

Today, scientists use electronic scanners, called CT scanners, to produce three-dimensional images of a mummy inside its bandages.

GLOSSARY

Afterlife
A life experienced after death. Different cultures have different beliefs about the afterlife.

Altar
A table, rock, or platform used in religious services

Artifact
A human-made object found at the sites of ancient homes or graves

Bacteria
Small, one-celled organisms. Some species cause disease or break down dead matter.

Curse
A wish or spell intended to cause harm to another person

Embalm
To use chemicals, perfumes, or ointments to preserve a body

Hieroglyph
(HIE-row-gliff)
A picture or symbol used to stand for a word or sound in ancient Egyptian writing

Monk
A man living and working in a religious community

Mummify
The process of making a body into a mummy

Mummy
A body that has been preserved by nature or by people

Natron
A naturally forming salt used by the ancient Egyptians to absorb fluids

Pharaoh
(FAIR-oh)
The title given to the kings of ancient Egypt who reigned from around 3000 BCE to 30 BCE.

Sacrifice
To kill a person or animal in a ceremony because of a belief that it will please a god

Shrine
A cabinet for holding a person's remains; also a place where people honor the memory of a dead person

Tomb
A grave, monument, or small building where a dead body is stored

Tutankhamun
(toot-an-kah-mun)
A boy pharaoh who ruled Egypt from about 1361 BCE to 1352 BCE

Underworld
The ancient Egyptians believed that everyone had to travel through this world beneath the earth on their journey to the afterlife.

X-rays
Special rays that are used to produce an image of a person's bones and internal organs

INDEX

afterlife
  artifacts 7, 19
  Egypt 9, 14, 15, 19
  Inca empire 27, 32
amulets 12, 13
Andes mountains 30
animal mummies 6
Anubis (Egyptian god)
  9, 14, 15
Ara, Pedro 40–42
Aramburu, Pedro 42, 43
Argentina 40–43
artifacts 7, 19, 20
bogs 6
brain 10–11, 45
Buenos Aires, Argentina
  40, 42
Cairo, Egypt 20, 21, 23
canopic jars 10–11
Carnarvon, Lord 18–19,
  22–23
Carter, Howard 16–23
cobras 20
CT scanners 45
curse of the mummy 16,
  20, 22–23
da Grubbio, Father
  Silvestro 38, 39
Duamutef (Egyptian god)
  11
Egypt 8–23
  afterlife 9, 14, 15, 19
  amulets 12, 13
  canopic jars 10–11
  cat mummies 6
  coffins 13, 15, 22
  gods and goddesses 9,
    10, 11, 14, 15, 19
  hieroglyphs 18
  jackal mask 9
  making a mummy
    8–15

pharaohs 16
scribes 14
Tutankhamun's tomb
  15, 16–25
embalming process
  Argentina 41–42
  Egypt 8, 9–13
  Sicily 39
Hapy (Egyptian god) 10,
  14
Hatshepsut (Egyptian
  queen) 23
hieroglyphs 18
Horus (Egyptian god) 11
Huari mummy 27
ice maiden 30–33
Imsety (Egyptian god) 11
Inca Empire 24–33
  afterlife 27, 32
  chica (drink) 28
  Cuzco 24, 29
  drought 32
  emperor mummies
    27, 28–29
  gods 24–25, 28, 32
  ice maiden 30–33
  Inti Raimi festival
    24–28
  llamas 26, 28, 30, 32
  map 24
  mummy x-ray 45
  sun temples 24, 28
Inti (Inca god) 24–25
Khepri (Egyptian god) 19
Koenig, Colonel Carlos
  42
llamas 26, 28, 30, 32
making a mummy
  Argentina 41–42
  Egypt 8–15
  Sicily 38–39
natron 11

naturally preserved
  bodies 6, 33
Nekhabet (Egyptian
  goddess) 19
Osiris (Egyptian god) 15
Palermo *see* Sicilian
  mummies
Perón, Evita 40–43
Perón, Juan 40, 41, 42, 43
Qebehsenuef (Egyptian
  god) 10
Roman mummies 6
Sapa Inca (emperor) 27,
  28
scientific studies 45
Sicilian mummies 34–39
  catacomb 34, 37, 39
  family visits 34, 36
  monks 36, 37
  mummification
    process 38–39
tomb robbers 15, 17
Tutankhamun (Egyptian
  pharaoh)
  coffins 22
  discovery of tomb
    16–17
  mummy 22
  search for tomb 15, 16
  tomb treasures 18–19,
    21–23
Valley of the Kings, Egypt
  15, 16, 17
wadjet eye 12
x-rays 12, 45

QUIZ

Answer the questions to see what you have learned. Check your answers in the key below.

1. What animals did ancient Egyptians believe were sacred?

2. True or False: Canopic jars were in the shape of different Egyptian gods.

3. What were wrapped in between the layers of a mummy's cloth?

4. The ancient Egyptian god Osiris was king of what?

5. What was Tutankhamun's final coffin made of?

6. What caused the Inca "ice maiden" to mummify?

7. On what Italian island were mummies kept in a catacomb?

8. What do scientists use mummies for?

1. Cats 2. True 3. Amulets 4. The afterworld 5. Solid gold
6. The freezing cold 7. Sicily 8. To find out what diseases people
suffered from in the past

KNIGHTS
AND CASTLES

FIRST EDITION

Series Editor Deborah Lock; **US Senior Editor** Shannon Beatty; **Editor** Radhika Haswani;
Senior Art Editor Ann Cannings; **Art Editor** Kanika Kalra; **Producer, Pre-Production** Nadine King;
Picture Researcher Sakshi Saluja; **DTP Designers** Neeraj Bhatia, Dheeraj Singh;
Managing Editor Soma Chowdhury; **Art Director** Martin Wilson;
Reading Consultant Linda Gambrell, PhD

THIS EDITION

Editorial Management by Oriel Square
Produced for DK by WonderLab Group LLC
Jennifer Emmett, Erica Green, Kate Hale, *Founders*

Editors Grace Hill Smith, Libby Romero, Michaela Weglinski;
Photography Editors Kelley Miller, Annette Kiesow, Nicole DiMella; **Managing Editor** Rachel Houghton;
Designers Project Design Company; **Researcher** Michelle Harris; **Copy Editor** Lori Merritt;
Indexer Connie Binder; **Proofreader** Larry Shea; **Reading Specialist** Dr. Jennifer Albro;
Curriculum Specialist Elaine Larson

Published in the United States by DK Publishing
1745 Broadway, 20th Floor, New York, NY 10019

Copyright © 2023 Dorling Kindersley Limited
DK, a Division of Penguin Random House LLC
24 25 26 27 28 10 9 8 7 6 5 4 3 2 1
001–341826–Mar/2024

A catalog record for this book
is available from the Library of Congress.
ISBN: 978-0-5938-4256-0

DK books are available at special discounts when purchased
in bulk for sales promotions, premiums, fundraising, or
educational use. For details, contact: DK Publishing Special Markets,
1745 Broadway, 20th Floor, New York, NY 10019
SpecialSales@dk.com

Printed and bound in China

The publisher would like to thank the following for their kind permission to reproduce their images:
a=above; c=center; b=below; l=left; r=right; t=top; b/g=background

123RF.com: andreykuzmin 24tl (shield), Jose Alfonso de Tomas Gargantilla 30tl, Anton Ivanov 37cra, Dmitriy Tereshchenko 28tl;
Alamy Stock Photo: Ann Ronan Picture Library / Heritage-Images / The Print Collector 29tr, Paul Doyle 37tr,
imageBROKER / GTW 41tr, The Picture Art Collection 27tr, 40tl; **Depositphotos Inc:** estebande 38bc; **Dreamstime.com:**
Andreykuzmin 31tr, Serhii Bobyk 24cla, Dauker 14cla, Dmitry 20tl, Ilkin Guliyev 22crb, Vladimir Korostyshevskiy 25tr,
Vladimirs Poplavskis 22tl, Srlee2 17tr, Lazarenka Sviatlana 22clb, Vladvitek 7tr, Vlastas 21tr, Jeff Whyte 44-45b, Witr 19tr;
Getty Images: Prisma / UIG 23tr; **Shutterstock.com:** Miguel Almeida 14crb, badahos 26cla, Danita Delimont 8tl,
Larisa Dmitrieva 38tl, IR Stone 18tl, Nicholas E Jones 42-43, Kozlik 24tl, Patrick Messier 44tl, St. Nick 4-5, ZGPhotography 6tl

Cover images: *Front & Spine:* **Shutterstock.com:** kontryphoto; *Back:* **Shutterstock.com:** Lemberg Vector studio cra

All other images © Dorling Kindersley

www.dk.com

Level

4

KNIGHTS ᴀɴᴅ CASTLES

Rupert Matthews

CONTENTS

6   Protecting the People

14   Great Castles of the World

22   Mighty Knights

30   Military Monks

38   Castles at War

46   Glossary

47   Index

48   Quiz

Castles Everywhere
During the Middle Ages, people built castles all across the world. A castle could only defend the land within a small area. So, rulers built multiple castles to expand their realms.

PROTECTING THE PEOPLE

Castles were built to show power and protect people during times of trouble. When danger threatened, people took their valuables into the castle until the danger had ended. During a war, a castle would be filled with people from the nearby farms seeking protection. Even in peaceful times, castles provided protection from bandits and criminals.

Most castles were built between the years 950 and 1500. This period of time is often called the Middle Ages or medieval period. The design of castles changed over the years. As new weapons were invented to attack castles, new methods of defense were developed, too.

Carisbrooke Castle, England
First built over 900 years ago, this castle has had many changes.

A Home, Too
A castle was also a home. A couple called the lord and the lady took care of a castle. During times of war and peace, they managed and protected their lands, their household, and the many people who served beneath them.

Fort or Fortress?
These castles don't look like what we might think of as castles. They were much simpler, but they could be built quickly to take control of the land.

Castles were often built on top of hills or beside rivers to make them more difficult to attack. Some castles were built beside a town to help defend it from enemies.

Early castles were made of wood and earth. A large mound of earth called a motte [MOT] was constructed up to 65 feet (20 m) tall and 200 feet (61 m) wide. On top of the motte was a wooden tower. This was the strongest part of the castle.

Walls in About a Week
These early castles could be built in just eight days.

9

How to Build a Motte-and-Bailey Castle

1. Choose the site for the castle.
2. Hire a master builder to design it.
3. Hire 300 workers to build it.
4. Dig the ditch around the bailey, and use the soil to build the bank.
5. Build a wooden wall around the bailey.
6. Build buildings in the bailey.
7. Dig a deep ditch around the motte, and pile up the soil to form the motte.
8. Build a tower on top of the motte.
9. Sit back and relax. You are now safe from your enemies.

Beside the motte, a large area of ground was surrounded by a ditch and a bank of earth. A wooden wall was built on top of the bank. This area was called the bailey. Several different buildings might be placed inside the bailey. Soldiers lived in barracks, while horses were kept in stables. The bailey might also include a church, offices, courthouse, workshops, kitchens, or a great hall.

During peaceful times, castles were used for many different purposes. People went there to pay their taxes or to obtain justice from the courts. Criminals would be kept in prison inside castles. Valuable goods would be kept inside the storerooms. More than a hundred people might live inside a castle.

After about the year 1100, the wooden walls and towers began to be replaced with stone. Defenses of stone were stronger and could not be set on fire so easily. Instead of a motte and tower, some castles had a massive square stone tower called a keep. The keep could be over 80 feet (24 m) tall.

Windsor Castle, England
The keep of this castle was rebuilt as the Round Tower in 1170.

Pricey Protection
Keeps were expensive and took many years to build.

Rochester Castle, England
Built in 1127, this tower keep has three floors.

Ready, Aim, Fire!
A catapult was a machine that could launch weapons like rocks or hot tar at a target. The chosen weapon, called the payload, was placed in a bowl-like area of the catapult called a bucket.

GREAT CASTLES OF THE WORLD

Soon, a new type of castle began to be built. Earth and wood were out. The new castles were made entirely of stone. They were some of the greatest castles ever built.

These new castles were safe. Their stone walls were tall enough to stop attackers on ladders from reaching the top. The walls were so thick that missiles thrown at them from catapults had no effect.

Scaliger Castle, Italy
From the top of these thick, high walls, guards could see across Lake Garda.

On top of the walls were rectangular openings called crenellations. Defenders could hide behind the tall parts of the wall or use their weapons through the gaps in between.

A Place to Hide
A castle's walls could also have wooden platforms that hung out over the side of the castle. The platforms were called hoardings. They had holes at the bottom that allowed defenders to drop heavy rocks onto attackers below without being seen.

The walls had tall, narrow holes in them called arrowslits. Guards standing inside could shoot arrows through the arrowslits. The openings were narrow to stop attackers shooting arrows back through them. Some openings had a short, horizontal slit to allow the guard inside a better view of the attackers.

Himeji [HIM-e-gee] Castle, Japan This fortified castle, also known as White Heron, was completed in 1609. It has more than 80 buildings spread out across multiple baileys. The buildings are connected by a series of gates and a maze of winding paths. A six-story tower stands in the center. The castle is surrounded by thick walls and a double moat.

arrowslit

Murder Holes
Tucked in the ceiling above the gatehouse, these openings allowed defenders to attack anyone who made it past the gatehouse.

Challenge Number One
A moat was the first obstacle that attackers would face when trying to invade the castle. To get past the watery trench, they would have to fill it with dirt or build bridges.

The gate in the outer wall was guarded by a gatehouse. A tall tower protected each side of the gate. A heavy grid of wood called a portcullis could be dropped to block the gateway.

A wooden platform called a drawbridge might cover a pit in front of the gate. The drawbridge was lifted when the gate was closed.

portcullis

Sometimes, a barbican was built outside the gatehouse. This building was like a small castle with walls and towers. Enemies had to capture the barbican before they could attack the gatehouse.

Many castles were surrounded by a deep trench called a moat. Some moats were flooded with water from a nearby stream or spring.

Fasil Ghebbi [fa–SIL ge–BI], Ethiopia King Fasil (Fasilidas) established this royal compound, which resembles a medieval European castle, as a permanent capital in 1636. Up until the 19th century, it served as the royal residence for Ethiopia's leaders. Over time, the compound grew to contain some 20 palaces and a host of other royal buildings.

moat

**Lal Qila
[lal KEE-la],
India**
This palace city,
called the Red
Fort, was built in
the middle of
the 17th century
by Shah Jahan,
one of the most
famous Mughal
emperors. It is
surrounded by—
and named for—
its massive, red
sandstone walls.

Later castles had lower walls
outside higher walls. These
are known as concentric castles.
Guards on the inner walls could
shoot arrows over the lower walls
at the enemy. If the attackers
captured the outer walls, the inner
walls were still above them.

Caerphilly [CAR-filly] Castle, Wales
Built between 1268 and 1271, this is the earliest
concentric castle in the UK.

Many castles had one tower that was taller and had thicker walls than the others. This was the keep or donjon [dun-jun]. It was the strongest part of the castle and would be the last section to be captured by attackers.

Forest Fortress
Château de Vincennes [VAHN-sen] in France had a donjon tower built around 1337. It is 170 feet (52 m) high.

Defensive Design
The high inner wall of Caerphilly Castle in Wales was surrounded by a low outer wall.

Brave in Battle
Knights were the medieval military. Charged with protecting a lord's castle, they had the most dangerous of jobs.

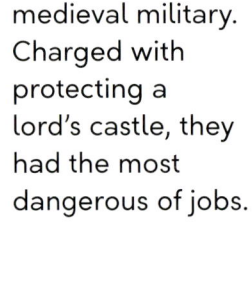

Weighty Warrior
As many as 200,000 iron rings were used to weave a knight's suit of chain mail armor. This metal mesh could stop a sword from slashing their skin.

MIGHTY KNIGHTS

In some parts of the world, honored warriors called knights defended kingdoms and did their ruler's bidding. When King Robert the Bruce of Scotland lay dying in 1329, he asked his trusted knight, Sir James Douglas, to take his heart on a trip to the Holy Land so it could be presented before God before it was buried.

After the king died, his heart was placed in a silver necklace that Douglas wore around his neck. But before Douglas and his company of knights could set out on their holy quest, they were sent to Spain to fight against Moorish armies. Douglas was killed during battle. He and the king's heart were returned to Scotland for burial.

The Moors
This medieval Muslim civilization originated in North Africa. In 711, the Moorish forces invaded the lands now known as Spain and Portugal. They ruled there until they were defeated, almost 800 years later. The Moorish culture—filled with art, science, technology, architecture, and learning—still influences the region today.

School Days
A boy left his home at about the age of seven to begin training for knighthood. He would become a servant, called a page, in a castle. Along with daily chores, he would get a basic education and learn manners. He would play with other pages and begin to learn how to battle.

During the Middle Ages, when castles were built, society was divided into three groups: the farmers and craft workers, the priests and bishops, and the king and his knights. The knights were organized in a strict order of importance. Squires were training to be knights, while bannerets were senior knights.

All knights were expected to obey a code of behavior known as chivalry [SHIV-al-ree]. Knights had to be brave in battle, but gentle in peace. They were supposed to protect the innocent and punish the guilty and be especially kind to women and children. Knights were expected to serve their king faithfully and respect the Church and God's teachings.

Sir John Chandos (c. 1314–1370) ———
Although not very good at fighting, Chandos was highly skilled at organizing an army.

The Norse
These fierce warriors came from Scandinavia. Children learned to fight from an early age. Wrestling was a favorite sport, and the Norse excelled at hand-to-hand combat. In battle, they fought with spears, axes, and swords. They used big, round, wooden shields for protection. The Norse were also excellent shipbuilders. They used their boats to conduct raids on other countries.

Some knights were not born into nobility. John Hawkwood was the son of a tanner in Essex. In about 1340, he became a soldier and joined the English army invading France. In 1356, he fought so well at the Battle of Poitiers that the King of England, Edward III, made him a knight.

When peace was arranged between England and France, Hawkwood formed a private army of unemployed soldiers, which he named the "White Company." Hawkwood marched his army into Italy and hired out his soldiers to whichever nobleman would pay him the most money. Hawkwood and his men made huge sums of money, and he married a wealthy duke's daughter.

A Head Start
It cost a lot of money to outfit a knight with armor, weapons, and a warhorse. That's why knights usually came from noble families who could handle the price tag.

Mighty Warrior
Tomoe Gozen was said to have been a female samurai, or *onna-musha*, during the 12th century. Known as a fearless and ruthless leader, she led a large army during the Genpei War.

The Samurai
From the 10th to the 19th centuries, Japanese feudal lords hired elite warriors called samurai. Samurai were skilled with both the bow and the sword.

Sir John Hawkwood (c. 1320–1394)
This is Hawkwood's funerary monument in Florence Cathedral, Italy.

"El Cid," meaning "The Lord," was the nickname of a heroic Spanish knight, Rodrigo Díaz de Vivar. He was born in 1040 into a noble family in the Kingdom of Castile. In 1065, King Sancho of Spain made El Cid his standard bearer. Carrying the flag, El Cid bravely and skillfully led the army into battle, fighting against the Moorish armies of southern Spain.

However, in 1081, the new king, Alfonso, quarreled with El Cid and sent him into exile. El Cid captured the Spanish city of Valencia [va-LEN-see-ah] in 1094 and declared himself ruler. When he was killed in battle in 1099, his wife, Jimena, had his body strapped to his horse so he could lead one last charge.

Charge!
Knights carried long spears called lances when fighting from atop their horses. When knights fell from their horses during battle, they had swords at the ready.

Rich Rewards
As payment for their military service, knights were given their own land and a noble title. Some of the most successful knights became more powerful than the lords they had served.

Rodrigo Díaz de Vivar (c. 1040–1099)
Rodrigo Díaz de Vivar, known as El Cid, was a Spanish knight who became a Spanish national hero.

MILITARY MONKS

Some castles were built for an unusual group of monks, who fought like knights. They were called the Military Orders of Monks.

In 1119, the French knight Sir Hugues de Payens found the bodies of a group of pilgrims near Jerusalem. They had been murdered by bandits on their way to the holy city.

Hugues founded a group of fighting monks called the Poor Fellow Soldiers of Christ. Their job was to patrol the roads to protect the pilgrims.

Code of Conduct
The Knights Templar followed a strict code of rules. They were not allowed to wear fancy clothes. Even shoelaces were forbidden.

King Baldwin of Jerusalem gave buildings on the Temple Mount in the city to them, and these monk-knights became known as the Knights Templar. For 200 years, they built castles, including the huge Kerak Castle, and fought battles in the Holy Land (now Israel).

Sacred Symbol
The symbol of the Knights Templar was a white shield with a red cross.

Kerak Castle, Jordan
Begun in 1132, it has cliffs on two sides.

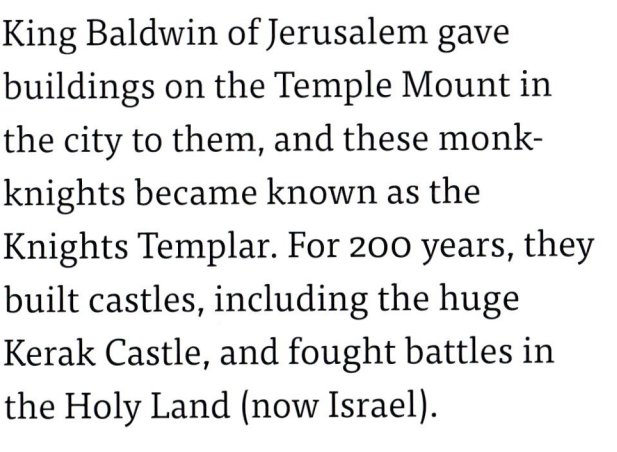

Warrior Teen
Joan of Arc (c. 1412–1431) was a French peasant with no military training. Yet she led the French army to a great victory in the city of Orléans. A few months later, she was captured in battle. She was tried and convicted of crimes against the Church. As punishment, she was burned at the stake. In 1920, she was named a Catholic saint. She is known as the Maid of Orléans.

Around the year 1120, the monks of the Order of St. John of the Hospital also took up arms to protect pilgrims to help them reach the holy sites. These Knights Hospitaller built many impressive castles to defend the route. Rebuilt in 1186, Margat Castle with its round towers perched on top of cliffs became their greatest castle.

Margat Castle, Syria
Also known as Marqab, this castle was triangular-shaped with a steep drop on one side.

The Knights Hospitaller also had a navy to protect pilgrims traveling by sea from attacks by pirates. They built castles on islands along the Mediterranean Sea as command posts, such as Kolossi Castle on Cyprus in 1254. They later ruled Malta until 1798, and today, they are based in Rome, Italy.

Kolossi Castle, Cyprus
Just one large tower now remains.

In 1190, the Order of Teutonic [too-TAH-nic] Knights was founded in Germany to protect pilgrims traveling to the Holy Land. In 1220, these knights bought the village of Mi'ilya and built Castellum Regis with its four massive square towers and a small church inside. In 1229, a tall narrow ridge became the site of Montfort Castle, their headquarters in the Holy Land.

Malbork Castle, Poland
This castle has been enlarged several times and now covers 52 acres, making it the world's largest castle.

From 1230 onward, the Teutonic Knights fought wars against people in eastern Europe who weren't Christian. Malbork Castle, now in Poland, was built in 1274 as their world headquarters. By 1400, the threat had disappeared, so the order became involved in charity work instead.

As well as the three great Military Orders, there were lots of smaller ones. The Order of Aviz was founded in 1146 to protect the Kingdom of Portugal against the Moorish armies. The Order of Calatrava fought from 1164 to 1490 to reconquer Spain from the Moorish troops. The Order of the Dragon was founded in Hungary in 1408 to fight the Turks.

Saone Castle, Syria
Saone Castle is thought to be one of the strongest castles in the world, but in 1188 it fell after a siege of just three days.

All of these Military Orders had a large role in the Crusades, which were religious wars between Christians and Muslims.

Armies from Christian countries in Medieval Europe felt that the city of Jerusalem and the surrounding Holy Land belonged to Christians. They waged war on the Muslim people who lived there. Crusaders rebuilt small forts, such as Saone [SONE] Castle in Syria, into huge, strong castles.

Beaufort Castle, Lebanon
Called the "Beautiful Castle," Beaufort was held by the Knights Templar until 1268.

Krak des Chevaliers [shuh-VAL-ee-ay], Syria
This castle began as a hilltop fortress. With walls up to 80 feet (24 m) thick, it was considered impossible to invade. The Knights Hospitaller rebuilt it into a great castle between 1142 and 1271.

Battering Ram
A tree trunk tipped in iron was placed on a wagon and wheeled forward to smash castle walls.

Slingshot
The trebuchet was a giant slingshot. It could hurl enormous rocks and barrels of hot tar as far as three American football fields.

CASTLES AT WAR

In 1136, Sir Baldwin de Redvers, Earl of Devon, rebelled against King Stephen of England. The king marched his army to lay siege to de Redvers's castle in Exeter. The king's army built a wooden castle to protect them, and they surrounded Exeter Castle to block supplies from reaching de Redvers and his people. The attackers used siege weapons to smash the walls of the outer bailey. They also dug a tunnel under the East Tower, causing it to collapse. De Redvers finally surrendered after dry weather caused the well to go dry.

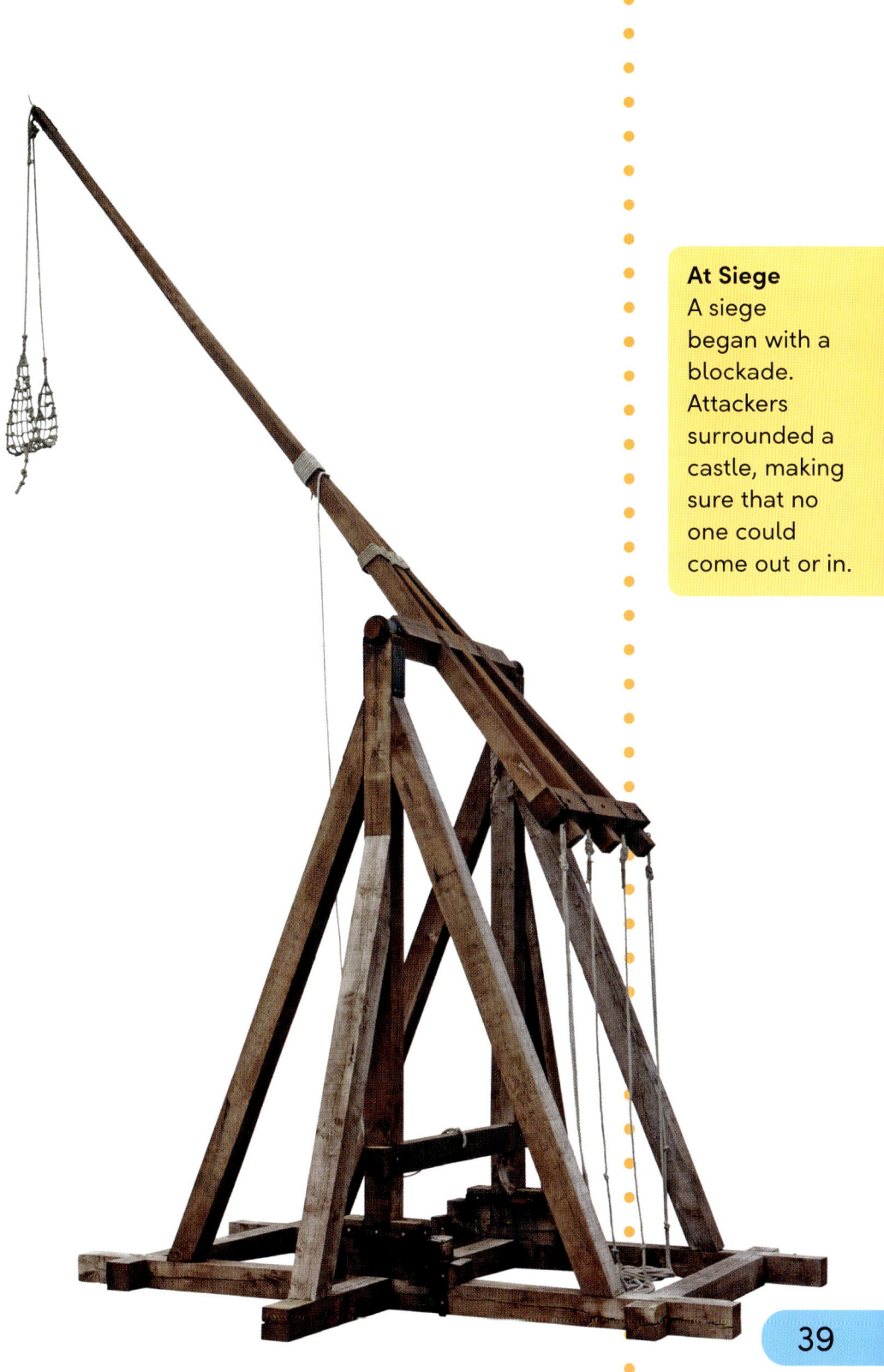

39

Nicola de la Haye Saves England

At a time when women had few rights, Nicola de la Haye inherited her father's land and his position as Constable of Lincoln Castle when he died. In 1217, French and English rebels overtook much of England. They tried to take Lincoln Castle. But, led by de la Haye, the castle did not fall. After reinforcements arrived, the attackers were defeated. This allowed the English king to remain on the throne.

A Long Battle
A siege could last months or even years.

When a siege took place, a castle became a very busy place. Hundreds of people from nearby farms and villages would come to the castle for safety, bringing their belongings. Tents and sheds were put up in the bailey along with large numbers of farm animals, carts, and tools.

The knight who owned the castle had to prepare for a siege. He brought huge amounts of food into the castle's storerooms. He made sure his soldiers had plenty of weapons and equipment. Riders on fast horses were sent out to look for the enemy approaching. When the enemy was seen, the gate was locked shut. No one could leave, and no further supplies could come in. The soldiers guarded the walls, ready to fight.

Water
Castles had containers called cisterns that could catch rainwater. This gave defenders under siege enough water to drink. Some castles had an underground well for water, too.

Supplying Provisions
This picture on a manuscript from the 1300s shows supplies arriving at a castle.

41

A Seven-Year Siege

The defenses of Harlech Castle in Wales were so strong that attackers tried to starve their targets into surrender. But supplies could still reach the castle by sea. The seven-year-long siege (1461–1468) only ended when an army of 10,000 men attacked and the outer defenses fell.

The siege of Kenilworth Castle lasted longer than most. It began in January 1266 when King Henry III attacked rebels led by Henry de Hastings. The wide moat surrounding the castle meant that the king's siege towers were useless and the catapults' stones could not reach the castle walls.

King Henry brought barges to carry his army over the moat, but they were sunk by the defenders of the castle. An effort to cross the water by raft also failed. Finally, an envoy from the Pope in Rome arranged a peace deal, and the rebels surrendered in December 1266.

Kenilworth Castle, England
This castle later became a splendid palace in the 1500s.

A Long History
Edinburgh Castle is the most besieged place in Great Britain.

Neither side in a fight ever wanted a siege to last long, but both wanted to win. In 1341, Scottish nobleman William Douglas set out to attack Edinburgh Castle, which was being held by the English. One night, Douglas led 1,000 soldiers to hide in trees near the castle. At dawn, 20 men pretending to be merchants drove a wagon to the castle. They said they brought food to sell.

The English opened the gates to let the "merchants" in. Dozens of Scottish soldiers were hiding in the cart. They leapt out to defend the gate and keep it open until Douglas arrived with his army to burst in and capture the castle.

Edinburgh Castle, Scotland
This castle was built on a tall volcanic crag.

GLOSSARY

Bandits
A group of robbers or people who break the law

Barbican
The tower and walls that form an outer defense of a castle

Catapult
A weapon that throws large stones

Concentric
[con-SEN-tric]
Circles of different sizes with the same center

Crenellations
[KREN-el-lay-tions]
Battlements with regular gaps

Envoy
A messenger or representative

Exile
Being unable to live in one's own country

Funerary
Used to remember a dead person

Headquarters
The main offices from where an organization is controlled

Horizontal
Flat or level, going from side to side

Moors
A group of Muslim people with African and Arab ancestry

Pilgrimage
A journey to a sacred place

Pilgrims
Religious people who travel to a sacred place

Pope
The leader of the Roman Catholic Church

Portcullis
[port-KULL-is]
A strong, heavy gate made from iron or wooden bars with points at the bottom, which hangs over a gateway into a castle

Siege
[SEE-j]
When an enemy surrounds a town or building, cutting off supplies and trying to force those inside to surrender

Standard
The flag of a royal family

Tanner
A person whose job is to make animal skins into leather

Taxes
Payment that has to be made to those in authority

Trench
A long, narrow hole dug out in the ground

Valuables
Small objects, such as jewelry, that belong to someone and are worth a lot to them

INDEX

arrowslits 17
attackers
   castle defenses 14,
     16–17, 20–21
   sieges 42, 44–45
bailey 10, 38, 40
bandits 6, 30
bannerets 24
barbican 19
battering ram 38
Beaufort Castle, Lebanon
   37
building a castle 10
Caerphilly Castle, Wales
   20
Carisbrooke Castle,
   England 7
catapults 14, 42
Chandos, Sir John 24
Château de Vincennes,
   France 21
chivalry 24
cisterns 41
concentric castles 20
crenellations 16
Crusades 37
de Hastings, Sir Henry 42
de la Haye, Nicola 40
de Redvers, Sir Baldwin
   38
defenses
   arrowslits 17
   barbican 19
   castle walls 20–21
   concentric castles 20
   crenellations 16
   hoardings 16
   keeps 12, 13, 21
   location 8
   moat 18, 19, 42
   murder holes 18
   stone towers and walls
     12, 14

donjon 21
Douglas, Sir James 22–23
Douglas, William 44–45
drawbridge 18
Edinburgh Castle,
   Scotland 44–45
El Cid (Rodrigo Díaz de
   Vivar) 28, 29
Exeter Castle, England 38
Fasil Ghebbi, Ethiopia 19
forts and fortresses 8
gatehouse 18, 19
Gozen, Tomoe 27
Harlech Castle, Wales 42
Hawkwood, Sir John 26,
   27
Henry III, King of England
   42–43
Himeji Castle, Japan 17
hoardings 16
Hugues de Payens, Sir 30
keeps 12, 13, 21
Joan of Arc 32
Kenilworth Castle,
   England 42–43
Kerak Castle, Jordan 31
Knights Hospitaller
   32–33, 37
Knights Templar 30, 31,
   37
Kolossi Castle, Cyprus 33
Krak des Chevaliers, Syria
   37
Lal Qila, India 20
lances 29
lord and lady 7
Malbork Castle, Poland
   34, 35
Mamluks 28
Margat Castle, Syria 32,
   33
Military Orders of Monks
   30–37

moat 18, 19, 42
monks 30–37
motte 8, 10, 12
murder holes 18
Moors 23, 28, 36
Norse 25
pilgrims 30, 32, 33, 34
portcullis 18
Robert the Bruce, King of
   Scotland 22
Rochester Castle, England
   13
Samurai 27
Saone Castle, Syria 36, 37
Scaliger Castle, Italy 15
siege 38–45
slingshot 38
soldiers
   barracks 10
   monks as 30
   private army 26
   sieges 41, 44–45
squires 24
standard 28
Stephen, King of England
   38
tanner 26
Teutonic Knights 34–35
towers
   barbican 19
   collapse 38
   gatehouse 18
   keeps 12, 13, 21
   motte-and-bailey
     castles 8, 10
   round towers 12, 32
   siege towers 42
   square towers 12, 34
Windsor Castle, England
   12

QUIZ

Answer the questions to see what you have learned. Check your answers in the key below.

1. What was used to make early castles?

2. Why were arrowslits narrow?

3. Where did the Moorish civilization originally come from?

4. What was the strongest part of a castle?

5. What was a deep trench that surrounded a castle called?

6. Who was asked to carry Scottish King Robert the Bruce's heart to the Holy Land?

7. Which military order of monks used Margat Castle?

8. True or False: Sieges always ended quickly.

1. Wood and earth 2. To stop attackers from shooting arrows back through the wall 3. North Africa 4. The donjon or keep 5. A moat 6. Sir James Douglas 7. Knights Hospitaller 8. False

GREEK
MYTHS

FIRST EDITION
Series Editor Deborah Lock; **Art Editor** Clare Shedden; **US Editor** John Searcy;
Production Editor Siu Chan; **Production** Erika Pepe; **Picture Researcher** Liz Moore;
Illustrators David Burroughs and Nilesh Mistry; **Reading Consultant** Linda Gambrell, PhD

THIS EDITION
Editorial Management by Oriel Square
Produced for DK by WonderLab Group LLC
Jennifer Emmett, Erica Green, Kate Hale, *Founders*

Editors Grace Hill Smith, Libby Romero, Michaela Weglinski;
Photography Editors Kelley Miller, Annette Kiesow, Nicole DiMella; **Managing Editor** Rachel Houghton;
Designers Project Design Company; **Researcher** Michelle Harris; **Copy Editor** Lori Merritt;
Indexer Connie Binder; **Proofreader** Larry Shea; **Reading Specialist** Dr. Jennifer Albro;
Curriculum Specialist Elaine Larson

Published in the United States by DK Publishing
1745 Broadway, 20th Floor, New York, NY 10019

Copyright © 2023 Dorling Kindersley Limited
DK, a Division of Penguin Random House LLC
24 25 26 27 28 10 9 8 7 6 5 4 3 2 1
001–341826–Mar/2024

A catalog record for this book
is available from the Library of Congress.
ISBN: 978-0-5938-4256-0

DK books are available at special discounts when purchased in bulk for sales promotions, premiums, fundraising, or educational use. For details, contact: DK Publishing Special Markets, 1745 Broadway, 20th Floor, New York, NY 10019
SpecialSales@dk.com

Printed and bound in China

The publisher would like to thank the following for their kind permission to reproduce their images:
a=above; c=center; b=below; l=left; r=right; t=top; b/g=background

Alamy Stock Photo: Artokoloro 40bl, Florilegius 12bl, Spencer Grant 28bl, Heritage Image Partnership Ltd / Historic England Archive 6tl, M.Brodie 9crb, Marcus Roberts Images / Stockimo 30br, SandraC 11tr, Zuri Swimmer 29bc; **Dreamstime.com:** Paradoks_blizanaca 31tr; **Getty Images:** De Agostini / DEA / G. DAGLI ORTI 21c, Hulton Archive / Heritage Images / Contributor 18cl; The J. Paul Getty Museum, Los Angeles: 32cl; **Library of Congress, Washington, D.C.:** LC-USZC4-10060 22tl; © **The Metropolitan Museum of Art:** Fletcher Fund, 1924 32tl, Gift of Mr. and Mrs. Leon Pomerance, 1953 45tr, Rogers Fund, 1921 7cr, 35cra; **Shutterstock.com:** Adwo 1bc, Dolfilms 25bl, Sergii Figurnyi 10tl

Cover images: *Front:* **Shutterstock.com:** Delcarmat ca, br, rudall30

All other images © Dorling Kindersley
For more information see: www.dkimages.com

www.dk.com

Level
4

GREEK
MYTHS

Deborah Lock

CONTENTS

6 Stories of Old

8 Family of Greek Gods

16 Pandora's Jar

20 Labors of Heracles

26 Theseus and the Minotaur

32 The Fall of Icarus

34 The Adventures of Perseus

40 The Foolishness of Midas

46 Glossary

47 Index

48 Quiz

The Written Word
The poets Homer, around 750 BCE, and then Hesiod, in 700 BCE, were the first people to write down Greek myths.

Telling Stories
The first Greek myths were told orally. The stories were passed down from one generation to the next.

Religion
Myths were an important part of the religion in ancient Greece.

STORIES OF OLD

In ancient times, the people of Greece built huge temples where they worshipped their gods and goddesses. Where did the idea of these gods come from? Like all cultures, the Greeks wanted to understand the changing seasons, the weather, why good and bad things happened to them, and what would happen when they died.

Temple of Poseidon

Belief in the Greek gods and goddesses spread throughout the ancient Greek empire.

Their answers lay in the belief that there were gods and goddesses, who took an interest in people's everyday lives. They told stories about these immortals. The stories, which we call myths, included tales of heroes, monsters, and spirits.

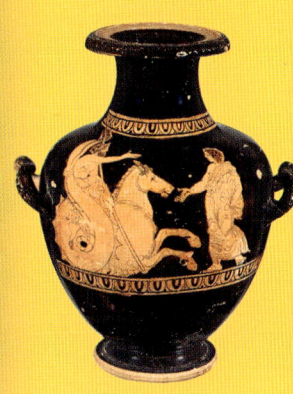

Greek Art
Myths were a popular subject in Greek art. Scenes from myths are depicted in ancient Greek sculptures and pottery.

Eros
The beautiful son of Aphrodite, Eros [AIR-oss], was the god of love. In myths, he was known for shooting his arrows at people to make them fall in love.

FAMILY OF GREEK GODS

Let's begin at the beginning with the god of the heavens, Uranus [YOUR-uh-nus], and the earth goddess, Gaia. Their children began the race of Titans, a group of powerful giants who roamed the heavens and earth. The youngest, Cronus, the god of time, took control when he killed his father. Aphrodite [af-ro-DIE-tee], the goddess of love, sprang from the sea as Uranus was cut into pieces.

Aphrodite, goddess of love and beauty

Cronus, god of time

Uranus, god of the heavens

Origins of the Gods
Uranus and Gaia had 12 children—six boys and six girls. These were the first generation of Titans.

Cronus had three sons: Zeus [ZOOS], Poseidon [puh-SIGH-dun], and Hades [HAY-deez]. He also had three daughters: Hestia, Demeter [de-MEE-ter], and Hera [HAIR-a]. It was these immortals and their children who appeared in many of the Greek myths.

Titanic
The word "titanic" comes from the Greek word *titanikos*, which means "big and powerful."

Zeus waged a terrifying war against his father and some of the Titans, and he defeated them. He then became the god of heaven and earth and went on to father many gods, goddesses, and heroes. He lived with his wife, Hera, along with Demeter, Aphrodite, and his eight immortal children on Mount Olympus, the highest mountain in Greece.

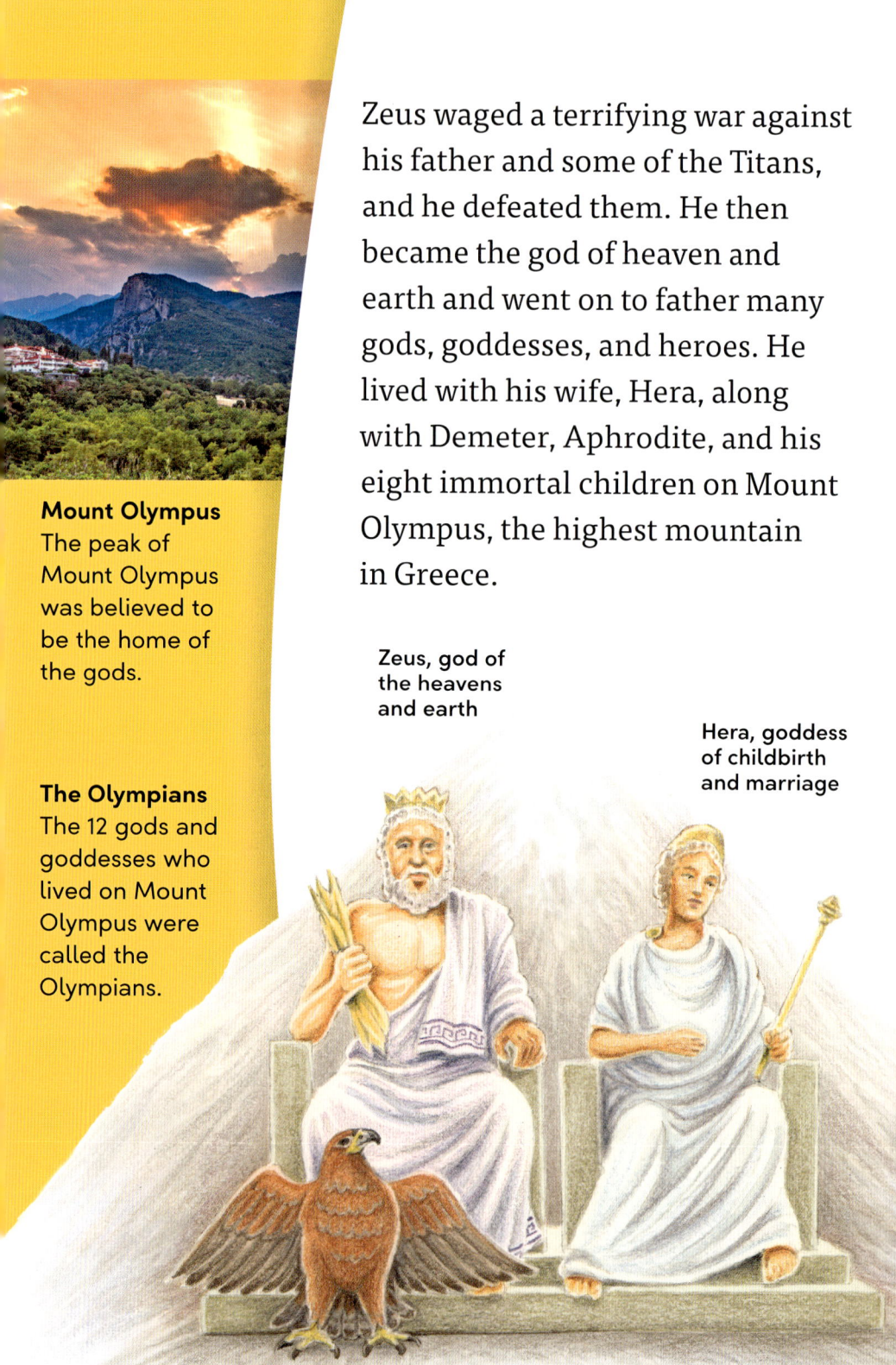

Mount Olympus
The peak of Mount Olympus was believed to be the home of the gods.

The Olympians
The 12 gods and goddesses who lived on Mount Olympus were called the Olympians.

Zeus, god of the heavens and earth

Hera, goddess of childbirth and marriage

Hestia, the goddess of the hearth and home, gave up her seat on Olympus to look after the fire within the mountain.

Poseidon, the god of the sea, lived in his golden underwater palace, stirring up storms and earthquakes if he was angry.

Poseidon, god of the sea

Hades was the dark god of the underworld—the place where people went when they died.

Hades, god of the underworld

Hestia
In the Greek language, "Hestia" means "hearth." In Greek society, the hearth, or fireplace, was the center of a home.

Poseidon
Poseidon held a three-pronged spear called a trident. It was created by one-eyed giants called the Cyclopes.

Hades
Hades was the name of the god of the underworld and the name of the dark place where he lived.

Sacred Site
Demeter stopped in Eleusis, a small town near Athens, while searching for Persephone. A temple there is dedicated to the goddess.

Demeter, the goddess of crops, had a beautiful daughter named Persephone [per-SEFF-uh-nee]. Hades kidnapped Persephone and made her his wife in the underworld. As Demeter grieved, the earth became frozen and nothing grew. Zeus ordered Hades to free Persephone.

Symbols attributed to Demeter include wheat and the Horn of Plenty.

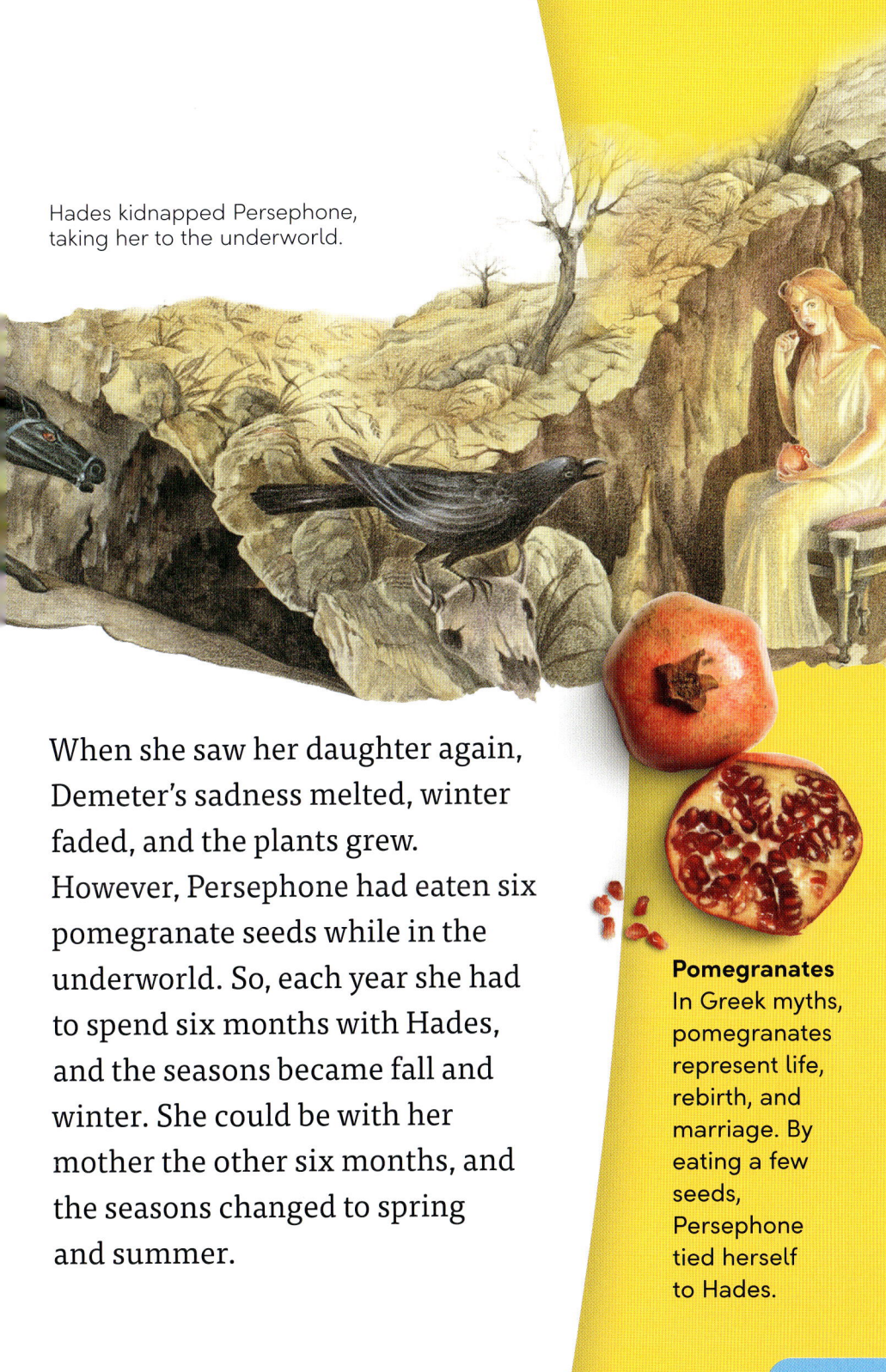

Hades kidnapped Persephone, taking her to the underworld.

When she saw her daughter again, Demeter's sadness melted, winter faded, and the plants grew. However, Persephone had eaten six pomegranate seeds while in the underworld. So, each year she had to spend six months with Hades, and the seasons became fall and winter. She could be with her mother the other six months, and the seasons changed to spring and summer.

Pomegranates
In Greek myths, pomegranates represent life, rebirth, and marriage. By eating a few seeds, Persephone tied herself to Hades.

13

Splitting Headache
Athena springs from Zeus's head.

Athena's City
Athens, the capital of Greece, was named for Athena after she won a competition against Poseidon.

Many of Zeus's immortal children had unusual birth stories. One day, Zeus had a bad headache. He asked his son Hephaestus [huh-FEST-uss] to split open his head with an axe. Out sprang Athena [a-THEE-na], dressed for battle and shouting her war cry.

Just like us, these titanic Olympians had emotions such as love, jealousy, and anger. They were fascinated by people and meddled in their lives with both heroic and fateful consequences.

Zeus and His Eight Immortal Children

Ares, god of war

Hebe, goddess of youth

Dionysus, god of wine and feasting

Artemis, goddess of the moon and wild animals

Apollo, god of light, music, and healing

Hermes, god of trade, and protector of travelers

Athena, goddess of wisdom and war

Hephaestus, god of the blacksmith's fire

PANDORA'S JAR

According to legend, Zeus wanted to create a race of people. He ordered Prometheus [pro-MEE-thee-us], one of the Titans, to mold men and women out of clay in the likeness of the gods. Zeus then breathed life into the people.

Prometheus
The name "Prometheus" means "forethought." Prometheus was a Titan. He saw that the Titans would only win the war against the Olympians with trickery. The Titans wouldn't listen to him, so he switched sides and helped the Olympians win.

Zeus, god of the heavens and earth

Prometheus lived among the people and taught them how to build homes, grow plants, and hunt animals. He begged Zeus to give them fire so they could cook and make metal tools, but Zeus refused.

"It will make them as powerful as the gods," he said.

However, Prometheus stole some fire from the rising sun. When Zeus saw the people using fire, he was very angry and severely punished Prometheus.

Eternal Punishment
For disobeying Zeus, Prometheus was chained to a high rock and had his liver torn out each day by an eagle. Since he was immortal, his liver grew back every night.

Hephaestus

Hephaestus was the Greek god of fire. He had forges throughout the Greek world, including one in his palace on Mount Olympus. He created weapons, armor, and gifts for the other gods.

Epimetheus

The name "Epimetheus" means "afterthought." While "Prometheus," meaning "forethought," is always a clever character in Greek myths, Epimetheus is always a fool.

Zeus also wanted to punish the people, so he asked Hephaestus to make a woman in his blacksmith's fire. The gods gave her gifts, such as beauty, love, curiosity, and deceit. They named her Pandora meaning "all-gifted."

She was sent to Prometheus's brother, Epimetheus [e-puh-MEE-thee-us]. She was also given a jar, which she was forbidden to open.

Pandora receives the gifts of beauty from Aphrodite, music from Apollo, and deceit from Hermes.

Pandora's Box
Even today, the term "Pandora's box" signifies a source of endless complications and troubles.

Although his brother had warned him not to accept a gift from Zeus, Epimetheus was enchanted with Pandora and married her.

Pandora could not forget about the jar. One day she peeked inside and all the evils flew out into the world—sickness, sin, and death.

As she closed the lid, hope was the only thing left in the jar.

Pandora

LABORS OF HERACLES

This is the tale of the greatest and strongest of all heroes—Heracles [HAIR-uh-kleez]. He was the son of Zeus, but his mother was a mortal woman. Hera was extremely jealous of Heracles. He grew into a determined, wise young man with superhuman strength and skills.

Zeus wanted his son to become a god when he died. Hera replied, "I will only agree to this if Heracles can perform 12 labors to be set forth by his cousin Eurystheus [you-RIS-thee-us], the king of Mycenae [my-SEE-nee]."

Superstrong

As Heracles lay in his cot, Hera sent serpents to kill him. Even though he was only a baby, Heracles strangled the serpents with his bare hands.

Eurystheus hated Heracles and hoped for his death. "Your first task is to kill the lion, which is devouring the people of Nemea," he commanded.

Heracles
Heracles was called Hercules by the Romans. Athena guided Heracles in many of his tasks.

Athena

Hercules Constellation

Hercules, based on the Roman adaptation of Heracles, is the fifth-largest constellation in the sky. It is one of the original 48 constellations identified by Ptolemy in the second century. It is visible in the Northern and Southern hemispheres.

The Nemean lion had skin that could not be pierced by weapons. So, Heracles followed the lion to its cave and wrestled with it. After strangling it to death, he returned to Eurystheus, wearing the lion's skin as armor. Heracles successfully completed task after task. His 11th task was to steal some golden apples that grew on a tree in a garden that was guarded by three maidens called the Hesperides [heh-SPARE-uh-deez], along with a fierce serpent.

After seeking advice from the gods, Heracles went first to the Hesperides' father, Atlas. Atlas was one of the Titans defeated long ago by Zeus. His everlasting punishment was to hold up the heavens on his shoulders. "If you ask your daughters for a couple of apples," offered Heracles, "I'll hold up the heavens for a while."

Herculean Tasks
Heracles' tasks included killing or capturing many of the fiercest mythical animals.

Atlas
The name "Atlas" in Greek can mean "suffering" or "very enduring."

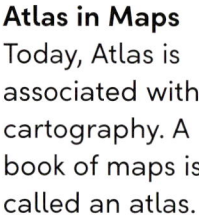

Atlas in Maps
Today, Atlas is associated with cartography. A book of maps is called an atlas.

Atlas agreed but asked Heracles to kill the serpent first. Heracles did this by shooting a single arrow over the garden wall. He then took up Atlas's burden. When Atlas returned with the apples, he did not want to take the heavens back.

"I'd be delighted to continue," said Heracles, "but could you just take them for a moment so that I can make a grassy cushion for my shoulder?"

When Atlas took the heavens back, Heracles picked up the apples and walked away. He then went on to complete his 12th labor. Zeus was pleased. When Heracles died, he joined the gods on Mount Olympus. He became the guardian of the door to the heavens.

Atlas in Art
Atlas is forever holding up the world on his shoulders in paintings, sculptures, and other works of art.

The Final Challenge
Heracles' 12th labor was to go to the underworld and bring back Hades' three-headed dog, Cerberus.

Greece

Crete

Legacy
The Minoan civilization, which existed on Crete, was named after King Minos.

King Minos
King Minos was one of the most famous kings in Greek mythology. He was a son of Zeus.

THESEUS AND THE MINOTAUR

Just off the coast of Greece is an island called Crete. It was here, say the myths, that a most fearsome creature called the Minotaur lived during the reign of King Minos. The Mintoaur was half-man and half-bull and ate only human flesh. The beast was so terrible that the king commanded his greatest craftsman, Daedalus [DED-uh-lus], to build a labyrinth that no one could escape from. At the center of this maze lived the Minotaur.

Every nine years, seven boys and seven girls were sent from Athens to be fed to the Minotaur. This was payment from the King of Athens, Aegeus [uh-GEE-us], for accidentally causing the death of Minos's son many years before. The third payment was now due.

Bulls of Knossos
When the ancient palace of Knossos in Crete was excavated, images of bulls were found. Some think this proves that the ancient Cretans worshipped bulls.

Maritime Messages

Colors and symbols on ship sails are commonly used to send messages. A white flag with a red X, for example, means "I need help!"

In Athens, the victims were being selected. A young prince named Theseus offered to go and kill the Minotaur. He was the adopted son of Aegeus and the son of the sea-god Poseidon.

The ship that Theseus took to Crete had black sails, but this time the crew took white sails with them.

"If you succeed, raise the white sails on your return," said Aegeus to his son.

When they arrived at Crete, the Athenians were met by King Minos and his daughter, Ariadne. She fell in love with Theseus at first sight.

"I'll help you kill the Minotaur if you take me back to Athens and make me your wife," Ariadne said to Theseus. He agreed.

Poseidon, god of the sea

Ariadne and Theseus

Theseus
Theseus volunteered to face the Minotaur so no more children of Athens would be eaten.

"Tie one end of this
magical ball of
thread to the entrance of
the labyrinth and follow it to the
center," Ariadne instructed. "Go at
night while the Minotaur sleeps.
After killing it, roll the thread
back up and it will lead you out."

That night, the glimmering
thread led Theseus to the
Minotaur, which he wrestled and
killed. When he arrived back at the
entrance, Ariadne and the Athenians
were waiting. They boarded their ship
and set sail for Athens.

On the way, Theseus left Ariadne asleep on the island of Naxos because he did not love her. He also forgot to change the sails from black to white. When King Aegeus saw the black sails, he thought his son was dead and threw himself into the sea. Theseus's triumphant return was overshadowed by grief.

King Aegeus
The body of water where King Aegeus died is now known as the Aegean Sea.

THE FALL OF ICARUS

King Minos was furious that Theseus had succeeded in defeating the Minotaur. He put the inventor of the labyrinth, Daedalus, and his lazy son, Icarus, into prison. Daedalus started planning how to escape.

He collected feathers from passing birds and made two pairs of wings by threading the feathers together and sealing them with wax from their candles. Finally, they were ready to escape.

Daedalus
An early type of Greek art was named after Daedalus. It is called Daedalic sculpture.

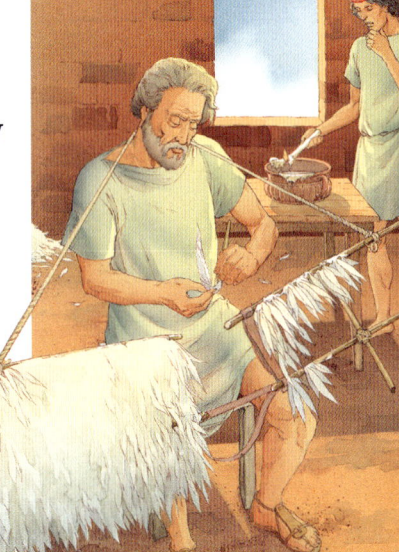

"Put on these wings," Daedalus told Icarus. "Follow me, and don't fly too high or too low."

They both took flight over the sea. Icarus was careful at first, but then soared upward, feeling free like a bird. The sun's heat then melted his wings and he tumbled to his death.

When Daedalus looked back for his son, he could see only feathers floating on the water.

Icarus
The part of the Aegean Sea where Icarus is said to have fallen is now known as the Icarian Sea. The island where his body washed ashore was named Ikaría.

Perseus
Perseus was the first Greek hero. In Greek myths, he lived several generations before Heracles was born.

THE ADVENTURES OF PERSEUS

There was a young man named Perseus, who lived with his beautiful mother, Danae [DAN-ay-ee], on the island of Seriphos [SEH-ri-fos]. The evil king, Polydectes, wanted to marry Danae, but Perseus protected her.

So, Polydectes tricked Perseus into attempting an impossible task. Polydectes held a feast. Being poor, Perseus came with no gift, but he promised the king a present.

"Bring me the head of the Gorgon Medusa," challenged Polydectes.

The Gorgons were three fearsome, scaly monsters, who had snakes for hair. Anyone who looked at Medusa's face turned to stone.

Medusa
The Gorgons were sisters. Unlike her sisters, Medusa was mortal and could be killed.

Nymphs

Nymphs were female spirits who protected natural things such as mountains, valleys, rivers, trees, wind, and rain.

Sickle

A sickle is a long, curved, metal blade with a short handle. It is a tool used in agriculture to cut tall grass or grain.

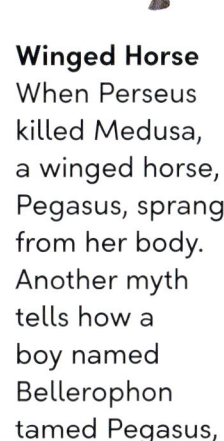

Perseus's father was none other than Zeus. From Olympus, Zeus sent Athena and Hermes to help his son. They gave him the shiniest shield and the sharpest sickle in the world.

Following their advice, Perseus then visited the nymphs of the North Wind. These female spirits loaned him some winged sandals, a leather bag, and Hades' Cap of Invisibility.

Wearing the sandals and cap, Perseus flew unseen to the far west where he found the three Gorgons asleep. Looking only at Medusa's reflection in the shield, he cut off her head with the sickle and put it into the bag.

Winged Horse
When Perseus killed Medusa, a winged horse, Pegasus, sprang from her body. Another myth tells how a boy named Bellerophon tamed Pegasus, using Athena's bridle.

The beheading of Medusa

As Perseus flew home, he saw a beautiful princess, Andromeda [an-DRAH-muh-duh], chained to a rock. Her parents had angered Poseidon and were sacrificing her to a sea monster to appease him.

As the monster rose from the waves, Perseus held up Medusa's head and turned it to stone.

Perseus married Andromeda and took her back to Seriphos.

King Polydectes had made Danae a slave and was surprised to see Perseus.

"Where's my gift?" he asked.

Without a word, Perseus held up the head of Medusa and turned the king to stone.

Story in the Stars
Several well-known star patterns have been named after the characters in Perseus's story. These include Perseus, Andromeda, her parents, and the sea monster.

THE FOOLISHNESS OF MIDAS

Not all myths are about heroes. Some tell of very foolish mortals who misused gifts from the gods. One such person was King Midas.

One day, Midas found an old satyr named Silenus in his garden. Silenus was drunk after feasting with the god Dionysus.

King Midas looked after Silenus very well and then returned him to Dionysus, who lived by the banks of the River Pactolus. In thanks, Dionysus promised Midas any gift he wanted.

"Let everything I touch turn to gold," replied Midas, greedily.

His wish was granted.

Mischievous Satyrs
Satyrs were roguish male spirits of nature who roamed the woods and mountains. They were half-man and half-goat and had horns, hooves, and tails.

Dionysus

Midas

41

King Midas
There may have been a real King Midas. In the eighth century BCE, King Mita ruled the kingdom of Phrygia, which is in modern-day Turkey. His kingdom was known for its gold and wealth.

With delight, Midas turned his palace and all the trees and flowers in his garden to gold.

However, his pleasure was short-lived. As he picked up food and drank his wine, they also turned to gold. Then, he hugged his daughter. To his horror, she turned to gold, too.

Midas returned to Dionysus and begged to be freed from his gift.

"Wash away your greed in the spring of the River Pactolus," Dionysus told him.

As Midas bathed in the river, the water turned to gold.

Still, Midas had not learned from his foolishness.

The Midas Touch
The term "Midas touch" is still used today to describe someone who succeeds at everything they try.

Pan

Midas

Tmolus

Apollo

Pan
People worshipped many Greek gods in temples. Because Pan was the god of nature, they worshipped him in caves.

Midas was a worshipper of Pan, the mischievous goat-like god of wild places. He enjoyed listening to Pan play country tunes on his reed pipes.

One day, Pan boasted that he was a better musician than Apollo, the god of music, and challenged him to a contest.

The contest was to be judged by the river god Tmolus [MO-lus]. Midas came along to listen and judge for himself.

Pan's merry tunes were no match for Apollo's lilting lyre music, and Tmolus awarded the prize to Apollo. However, Midas said he preferred Pan's playing. In anger, Apollo gave Midas a pair of long, hairy donkey ears. Midas covered his ears in a turban, but people found out about them and he died of shame.

Lyre
A lyre is a U–shaped harp. In ancient Greece, singers and poets were often accompanied by lyre music when they performed.

GLOSSARY

Excavate
To dig up something of historical interest

God
A male immortal with power over nature and human affairs, who is believed in and worshipped by people

Goddess
A female immortal with power over nature and human affairs, who is believed in and worshipped by people

Gorgons
Three frightening female creatures with snakes for hair and golden wings

Hero
A mortal who is known for doing great deeds

Immortal
A supernatural being that lives forever

Labor
A task that requires great effort

Labyrinth
A difficult maze big enough for people to walk through

Mortal
A person who will die someday

Mount Olympus
The highest mountain in Greece. The ancient Greeks believed their gods and goddesses lived on the peak.

Myth
A traditional story about supernatural beings and heroes

Nymphs
Minor goddesses of nature written about in myths

Pegasus
A winged horse that sprang from the body of Medusa

Pomegranate
A hard, red fruit about the size of an orange, containing many large seeds within a juicy, red pulp

Satyr
A half-human, half-animal woodland god

Superhuman
Having greater abilities than a normal person

Temple
A place where gods and goddesses are worshipped

Titans
A family of giants featured in Greek myths

Underworld
The place where ancient Greeks believed they would go when they died

INDEX

Aegeus, King of Athens 27, 29, 31

Andromeda 38–39

Aphrodite 8, 10, 18

Apollo 15, 18, 44–45

Ares 15

Ariadne 29–31

Artemis 15

Athena 14, 15, 21, 37

Athens, Greece 14, 27, 29, 30

Atlas 23–25

Bellerophon 37

Cerberus 25

constellations 22, 30, 39

Crete 26, 27, 29

Cronus 8, 9

Cyclopes 11

Daedalus 26, 32–33

Danae 34, 39

Demeter 9, 10, 12–13

Dionysus 15, 40, 41, 43

Eleusis 12

Epimetheus 18–19

Eros 8

Eurystheus, King of Mycenae 20–21, 22

Gaia 8, 9

Gorgons 35, 37

Hades 9, 11, 12–13, 25, 37

Hebe 15

Hephaestus 14, 15, 18

Hera 9, 10, 20

Heracles 20–25

Hermes 15, 18, 37

Hesiod 6

Hesperides 22, 23

Hestia 9, 11

Homer 6

Icarus 32–33

immortal 7, 9, 10, 14, 15, 17

labyrinth 26, 30, 32

lyre 45

Medusa 35, 37, 38, 39

Midas, King 40–45

Minos, King of Crete 26–27, 29, 32

Minotaur 26–30, 32

Mita, King of Phrygia 42

Mount Olympus 10–11, 18, 25, 37

Naxos 31

Nemean lion 21–22

Nereids 38

nymphs 36, 37, 38

Olympians 10, 14, 16

Pan 44–45

Pandora 18–19

Pegasus 37

Persephone 12–13

Perseus 34–39

Polydectes, King of Seriphos 34–35, 39

pomegranates 13

Poseidon 9, 11, 14, 29, 38

Prometheus 16–19

Ptolemy 22

satyrs 40, 41

seasons 13

sickle 36, 37

Silenus 40–41

temples 6, 12

Theseus 29–31, 32

Titans
  Atlas 23–25
  Epimetheus 18–19
  family of gods 8, 9, 10
  Prometheus 16–19

Tmolus 44, 45

underworld 11, 12–13, 25

Uranus 8, 9

Zeus
  children 10, 14, 15, 20, 25, 26, 37
  family of gods 9, 10, 12, 14
  Pandora's jar 16–19

QUIZ

Answer the questions to see what you have learned. Check your answers in the key below.

1. Which Greek god led the fight against the Titans?

2. Why are the Greek gods called Olympians?

3. How did Pandora come to be?

4. How many labors did Heracles have to complete?

5. What was Theseus's great accomplishment?

6. Why did Icarus fall from the sky?

7. What kind of creature was Medusa?

8. Which Greek god gave King Midas the golden touch?

1. Zeus 2. They live on Mount Olympus 3. Prometheus made her in his blacksmith's fire 4. 12 5. He killed the Minotaur 6. He flew too close to the sun and his wax wings melted 7. A Gorgon 8. Dionysus

FIRST
FLIGHT

FIRST EDITION
Project Editor Caroline Bingham; **Art Editor** Helen Chapman; **Series Editor** Deborah Lock;
Senior Art Editor Cheryl Telfer; **US Editor** Beth Hester; **DTP Designer** Almudena Díaz;
Production Shivani Pandey; **Picture Researcher** Bridget Tily; **Illustrator** Peter Dennis;
Jacket Designer Dean Price; **Indexer** Lynn Bresler; **Curatorial Reviewer** Peter Jakab;
Reading Consultant Linda Gambrell, PhD

THIS EDITION
Editorial Management by Oriel Square
Produced for DK by WonderLab Group LLC
Jennifer Emmett, Erica Green, Kate Hale, *Founders*

Editors Grace Hill Smith, Libby Romero, Michaela Weglinski;
Photography Editors Kelley Miller, Annette Kiesow, Nicole DiMella; **Managing Editor** Rachel Houghton;
Designers Project Design Company; **Researcher** Michelle Harris; **Copy Editor** Lori Merritt;
Indexer Connie Binder; **Proofreader** Larry Shea; **Reading Specialist** Dr. Jennifer Albro;
Curriculum Specialist Elaine Larson

Published in the United States by DK Publishing
1745 Broadway, 20th Floor, New York, NY 10019

Copyright © 2023 Dorling Kindersley Limited
DK, a Division of Penguin Random House LLC
24 25 26 27 28 10 9 8 7 6 5 4 3 2 1
001–341826–Mar/2024

A catalog record for this book
is available from the Library of Congress.
ISBN: 978-0-5938-4256-0

DK books are available at special discounts when purchased in bulk for sales promotions, premiums,
fundraising, or educational use. For details, contact: DK Publishing Special Markets,
1745 Broadway, 20th Floor, New York, NY 10019
SpecialSales@dk.com

Printed and bound in China

The publisher would like to thank the following for their kind permission to reproduce their images:
a=above; c=center; b=below; l=left; r=right; t=top; b/g=background

Shutterstock.com: Evannovostro 20tl

Cover images: *Front:* **Alamy Stock Photo:** RGB Ventures / SuperStock / Library of Congress

All other images © Dorling Kindersley
For more information see: www.dkimages.com

www.dk.com

Level

4

FIRST
FLIGHT

Caryn Jenner

CONTENTS

6 Flying Machines

8 The Toy Helicopter

12 Brothers in Business

14 The Bicycle Boom

18 Aiming for the Sky

22 Flying Experiments

32 The Wright Flyer

40 Flying Far

46 Glossary

47 Index

48 Quiz

Icarus

In the ancient myth, the Sun melted Icarus's wings and he fell into the sea. Some people saw this as a warning that humans were not meant to fly.

Leonardo da Vinci

This model of an ornithopter is based on sketches by the Italian artist and scientist Leonardo da Vinci.

FLYING MACHINES

Today, air travel is commonplace, thanks to the amazing invention of Wilbur and Orville Wright. But in past centuries, people could only imagine what it would be like to fly.

An ancient Greek myth tells the story of Daedalus and Icarus, who made wings from feathers and wax.

Much later, others, such as Leonardo da Vinci, tried to invent flying machines. In the 15th century, da Vinci designed a machine with enormous flapping wings, and had ideas for a helicopter and a parachute. However, his machines would not have been able to fly. He thought that the flapping wings of a bird held the key to human flight.

In 1783, the Montgolfier brothers from France invented the hot-air balloon.

Because the hot air in a balloon is lighter than the cold air around it, the balloon rises. The hot-air balloon is a "lighter-than-air" flying machine.

In the first half of the 1800s, Sir George Cayley became a true pioneer in the science of flight. He designed the first glider. At the end of the century, Otto Lilienthal flew his own gliders, although his flights were unsteady and brief. It was up to Wilbur and Orville Wright to make the dream of flight a reality.

Montgolfier Balloon
The hot-air balloon allowed people to look down from the sky for the first time.

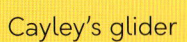

Cayley's glider

THE TOY HELICOPTER

DATE 1878

Wilbur and Orville Wright couldn't wait to see the surprise their father had brought home for them.

"Here it is, boys!"

Their father tossed a small toy into the air. Instead of falling, the toy rose up toward the ceiling. Wilbur and Orville watched in amazement.

"It flies!" exclaimed Orville.

"But how does it fly?" Wilbur wondered.

The two brothers studied the toy helicopter and discovered that it was powered by twisting a rubber band. As they let the helicopter go, the rubber band unwound, causing the propeller to spin quickly and the helicopter to fly in the air. As the propeller slowed down, the helicopter wobbled, then fell to the ground.

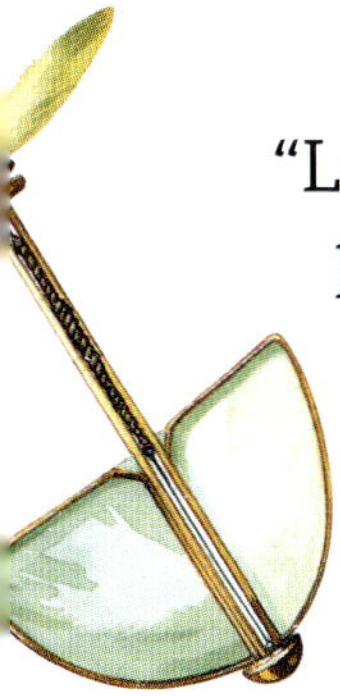

"Let's make our own helicopters, Orville," Wilbur suggested.

So the boys experimented with their own versions of the toy helicopter. They found that the bigger the helicopter was, the quicker it fell to the ground.

Later, while inventing the first airplane, the Wright brothers would remember the toy helicopters that were their first flying machines.

Rubber Band
When you stretch or twist a rubber band, it uses force in order to spring back to its usual size. The brothers' helicopter used a twisted rubber band at its center. The boys called their toy helicopters "bats."

Woodcuts
To make a woodcut, Orville carved a picture into a block of wood. Then he dipped the wood into some ink and printed the picture onto a piece of paper.

As they grew up, the Wright brothers could often be found making things and experimenting.

Wilbur invented a machine to fold the newspapers that his father sent around the United States.

Orville loved to make and fly kites. He even made kites to sell to his friends. He was also interested in printing with woodcuts.

The boys' parents, Milton and Susan Wright, encouraged their curiosity. They wanted their children to learn as much as they could, and the house was filled with books.

Unlike most women in the 1800s, Susan had gone to college. Milton was a minister who traveled around the country. He also edited a religious newspaper.

Wilbur and Orville had two older brothers and a younger sister, but the two younger boys were especially close. Wilbur once said, "From the time we were little children, my brother Orville and myself lived together, worked together, and, in fact, thought together."

Throughout their lives, the brothers worked as a team.

Susan Wright
The boys' mother was handy with tools, and often built things for the children.

Milton Wright
Their father wrote many letters home telling his family about the places he visited.

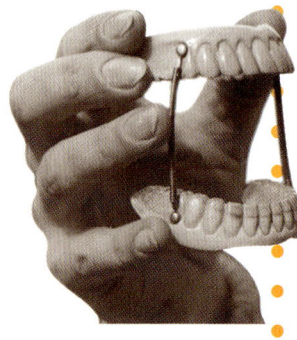

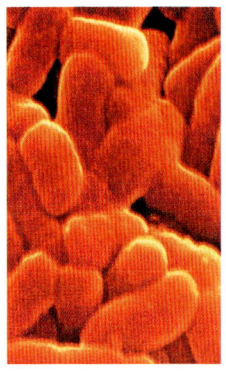

BROTHERS IN BUSINESS

DATE 1884

The Wright family moved back to Dayton, Ohio, where they had once lived.

Orville owned a small printing press. Wilbur was looking forward to going to college. But during a hockey game, a player hit him in the face with a hockey stick. Several of Wilbur's teeth were knocked out, and he had to with false ones.

The injuries healed, but Wilbur lost his confidence and became very quiet. He decided not to go to college after all.

At the same time, Susan Wright was suffering from a lung disease called tuberculosis. She died in 1889. The entire family mourned, but Wilbur was particularly close to his mother, and he felt very upset.

Orville thought that Wilbur needed something to keep him busy. He asked his brother to help him start a newspaper called the *West Side News*. Wilbur enjoyed writing for this and other newspapers that the brothers published. He had always followed current affairs, but now he paid special attention. He wrote articles in support of women's right to vote and other main issues.

WEST SIDE NEWS

Vol. I. DAYTON, OHIO, MARCH 1, 1889. No. I.

West Side News.

PUBLISHED WEEKLY.

Orville Wright - - - Publisher.

TERMS:—One year, forty cents. Ten weeks, ten cents.

DAYTON, OHIO.

Sherman and Lincoln.

General Sherman makes no secret of the fact that his first impressions of President Lincoln were decidedly unfavorable. He came to know him better before very long, however, and describes with evident satisfaction a visit which the President made to the Army of the Potomac soon after the battle of Bull Run.

General Sherman, or Colonel Sherman, as his title then was, asked Mr. Lincoln if he intended to speak to the men, and volunteered to add that he hoped he would discourage all cheering and

Mr. Lincoln, still standing, replied: "Threatened to shoot you?"

"Yes, sir, he threatened to shoot me."

The President looked at the soldier and then at the colonel, and then, stooping toward the soldier, said, in a loud stage-whisper, audible for quite a distance:

"Well, if I were you, and Colonel Sherman threatened to shoot me, I wouldn't trust him, for I believe he would do it."

The complainant disappeared amid the laughter of the men, and the President remarked to the colonel:

"Of course I didn't know anything about the case, but I thought you knew your business best."
—*Youth's Companion.*

LAWYER.
I slept in the editor's bed last night,
When no other chanced to be nigh,
And I thought, as I tumbled the editor's bed,
How easily editors lie!

EDITOR.
If the lawyer slept in the editor's bed,

ceed three thousand men, whereupon Washington moved as an amendment, that no enemy should ever invade the country with over two thousand men.

HOLLINGER
IS THE
PHOTOGRAPHER,
Cor. Third and Jefferson.

Opera Glasses to Rent.
Prices very low, at
H. C. RUFF'S,
1032 West Third St., Dayton, O.

TRUNKS,
TRAVELING BAGS.
Shawl Straps, Grips,
MUSICAL INSTRUMEMTS,
Gloves and Whips

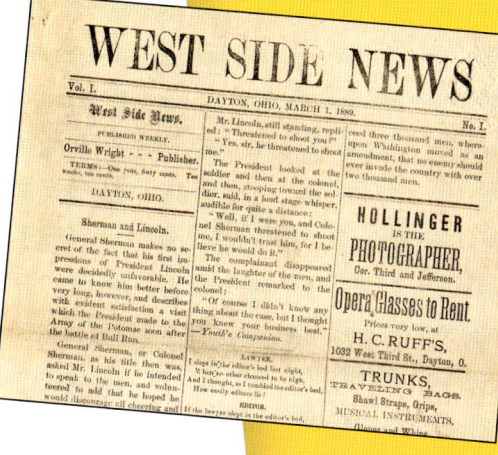

Newspapers
The slogan for the Wright brothers' newspapers was: "All the news of the world that most people care to read, and in such a shape the people will have time to read it."

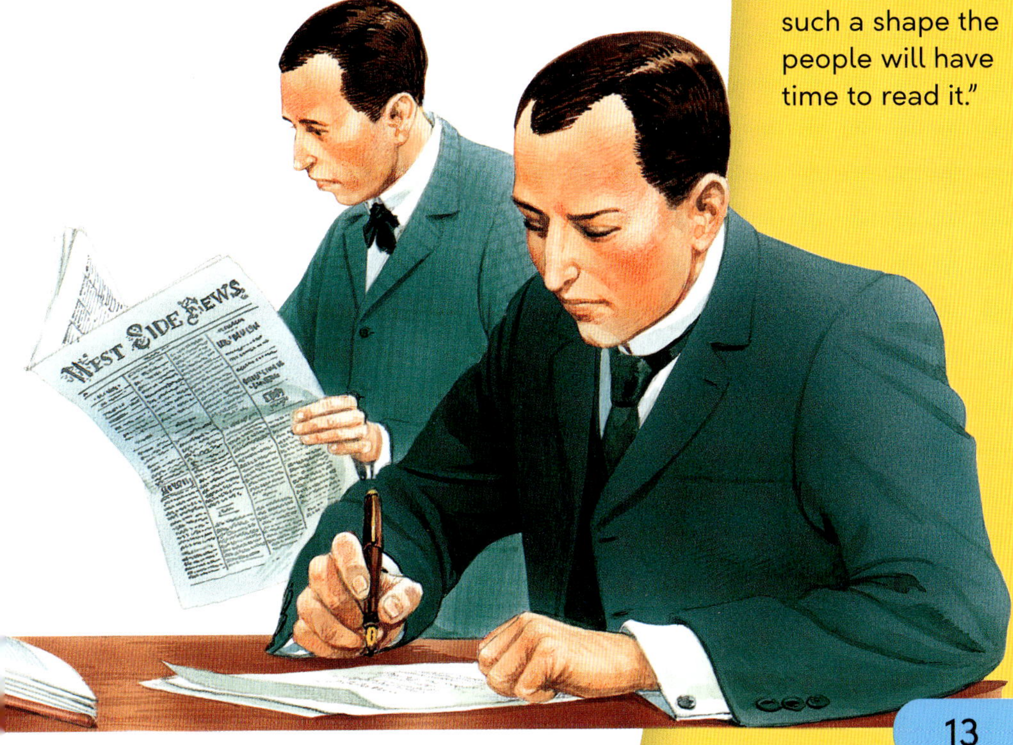

THE BICYCLE BOOM

DATE 1892

The Wright brothers found a new interest when Orville bought a safety bicycle.

It was called a safety bicycle because the front and back wheels were the same size, so it was safer to ride than the old-style "high-wheel" bicycles.

"I feel like I'm flying!" Orville called to Wilbur, as he zoomed past on his new bike.

Soon, Wilbur bought a safety bike, too. In fact, the invention of the safety bicycle started a craze for cycling. Like many bicycle enthusiasts of the time, the Wright brothers joined a cycling club.

They went for bicycle rides in the countryside with the club, and Orville even won some races.

The Wright brothers were also skilled at repairing bicycles. Soon, cycling enthusiasts in Dayton were bringing their bikes to Wilbur and Orville to be fixed. The brothers saw a new business opportunity. They opened a bicycle repair shop.

SPRINGFIELD BICYCLE CLUB.

BICYCLE CAMP-EXHIBITION & TOURNAMENT.
SPRINGFIELD, MASS., U.S.A. SEPT. 18, 19, 20, 1883.

Bicycle Clubs
Cycling was also called "wheeling." It was a fun method of travel for both men and women, and it was also a popular social activity.

The Wright brothers' cycle shop

Van Cleve
The Van Cleve bicycle was named after an Ohio pioneer who was related to the Wright family.

The Wright Cycle Company became a thriving business. As well as repairing bicycles, Wilbur and Orville began making bikes to sell. They ordered parts from bicycle factories, then fitted them together to their own designs, making improvements. They called their special models the St. Clair and the Van Cleve.

By 1896, there was another new form of transportation on the streets of Dayton. The brothers' friend, Cord Ruse, built the first automobile in town.

"Why fiddle with bicycles when you can have a horseless carriage?" called Cord, as his car sputtered and clanked outside the Cycle Company. "I just fill it with gas and off it goes."

Orville laughed. "Just don't lose any of those nuts and bolts I hear rattling around."

"You should attach a big bed sheet under the engine to catch those loose parts, Cord," added Wilbur.

Cars did not have the same attraction for the Wright brothers that bicycles did and neither brother believed that cars would catch the public's imagination. But there was another form of transportation that would soon begin to fascinate them—flying machines.

The Horseless Carriage
A "horseless carriage" was another name for a car. Early cars were noisy and dusty, and often unreliable.

Gas
The Wright brothers used gas to fuel the engines of their airplanes.

Otto Lilienthal
Otto Lilienthal made over 2,000 glider flights, but he had limited control of the glider.

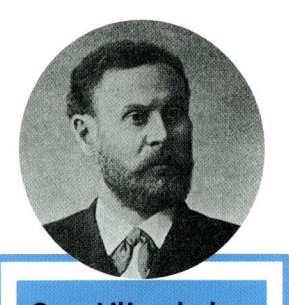

AIMING FOR THE SKY

DATE
1896

Wilbur read about the death of Otto Lilienthal, a German glider pilot. Lilienthal had died when his glider crashed. The brothers admired the pilot's accomplishments in his glider. Once again, their thoughts turned toward the challenges of flight.

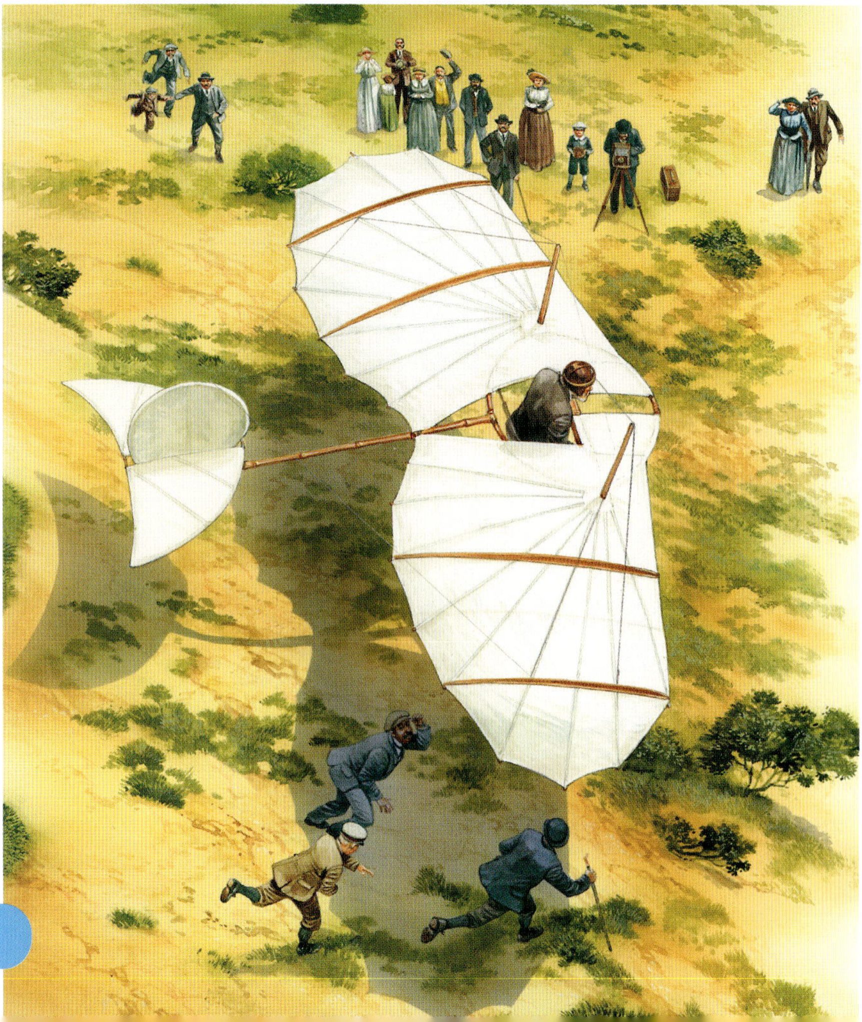

They decided that a practical flying machine had three main requirements. First, the pilot had to be in control of the aircraft. Second, the design of the wings had to provide lift for the aircraft. Third, an aircraft had to be powered by an engine so that the aircraft could stay up for a long time.

For the next few years, Wilbur and Orville learned all about the different types of flying machines that had already been attempted. They learned about birds and observed them flying.

Wilbur and Orville decided to experiment with a biplane, and focus on a way to control the aircraft before they added an engine.

"Birds only have to twist their wings slightly in order to control their flight," said Orville.

"We might be able to control our aircraft if we can find a way to twist the wings," said Wilbur. "But how?"

Biplane
A biplane is an aircraft that has two wings, one on top of the other. The Frenchman Louis Blériot was the first to experiment with a monoplane—a one-wing aircraft.

Bird Flight
The flight of birds is very complicated. The flapping of the wings, and the opening and closing of the feathers to push against the air or let the air slip through helps the bird to lift, swoop, and soar.

Box Twisting
Wilbur imagined that the box was twisting like the parallel wings of a biplane.

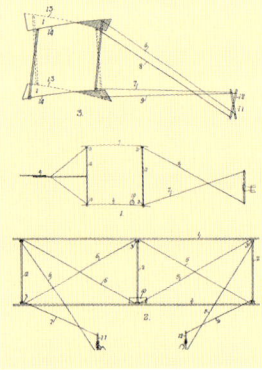

Kite Sketch
Wilbur's sketch shows how the wings twist slightly, like the wings of a bird.

DATE 1899

One summer day, Wilbur was working in the bicycle shop. As he absent-mindedly twisted the ends of a long, thin box, he had an idea.

The brothers made a large biplane kite. Ropes ran from the front corners of the wings to two sticks that were used to control the kite from the ground. When the sticks were tugged, the corners of the wings twisted slightly, changing the direction of the kite. This twisting mechanism became known as wing-warping.

Wilbur tested the kite while Orville was camping with friends. It swooped and soared like a bird. A group of people watched him curiously.

Wilbur made the kite dive so low that the people had to duck to avoid it. Just in time, he used the control sticks to twist the wings and the kite soared into the air.

Wilbur cycled all the way to the campsite to show Orville. It was the breakthrough they needed.

Wilbur's Kite
Wilbur's kite had a five-foot (1.5-m) wingspan. The wings were made of a fabric-covered wooden structure, with wooden struts to hold the kite together.

Weather Bureau
The Weather Bureau keeps records of weather patterns around the country. With the development of satellites, they can also predict weather.

Kitty Hawk
Along with its advantages, Kitty Hawk also had disadvantages, such as sandstorms caused by the strong winds.

FLYING EXPERIMENTS

DATE 1900 The brothers spent about a year making their first glider. It was based on their kite, but much bigger, with wings that were 17 feet (5 m) long from tip to tip. They added a flat section at the front of the lower wing, called an elevator. The pilot would lie down on the wings.

The Wright brothers would need a windy place to test their glider.

After studying information from the United States Weather Bureau, they decided on Kitty Hawk, an isolated fishing village on the coast of North Carolina.

Kitty Hawk was an excellent testing site in many ways. Along with steady winds, there were tall sand dunes to help launch the glider, few buildings or trees to crash into, and open stretches of sand to cushion any falls. There were also very few people, so the Wright brothers could conduct their experiments without publicity.

Elevator
One reason for placing the elevator at the front was the protection it would provide in case of a crash.

Packing

Wilbur and Orville had built the glider in Dayton, then taken it apart and packed the pieces into crates that Wilbur took with him.

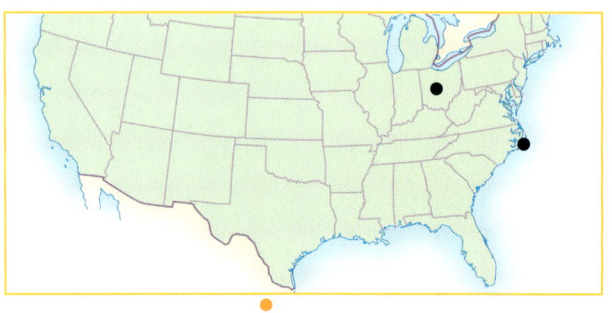

Train

As the Wright brothers were beginning to experiment with flight, there were big advances in train systems. Electric trains were beginning to make an appearance.

Wilbur left for Kitty Hawk in early September while Orville sorted things out at the bicycle shop. Wilbur took with him most of the parts for the glider and the tools needed to assemble it. He also took a large tent.

Wilbur's journey from Dayton to Kitty Hawk began with a 24-hour train ride. Then he took a ferry, and then another train. Finally, he hired a fisherman to take him the rest of the way in his boat.

A few hours after setting sail, the boat got caught in a severe storm. In the dark of night, huge waves bounced the tiny boat.

Fierce winds ripped the sails. The fisherman had to anchor the boat in a sheltered cove for the night. Wilbur slept on the hard deck. The storm passed, and Wilbur arrived in Kitty Hawk late the following night.

In all, it took Wilbur nearly a week to get there. But the trip would lead to a new—and much faster—form of transportation.

Wilbur outside the tent

Tom Tate

Tom Tate was the nephew of Kitty Hawk's postmaster. Orville said that Tom could "tell more big yarns than any kid of his size I ever saw."

The brothers began by flying the glider like a kite. The glider was large, and the controls took practice to master. Within three days, it crashed! Although disappointed, the brothers soon repaired it.

Sometimes a local boy named Tom Tate rode the glider while the brothers controlled it from the ground. Sometimes Wilbur flew the glider himself.

The brothers realized that in order to fly better, the glider needed more upward movement, or lift.

The following summer, in 1901, they returned to Kitty Hawk with a new glider. Flight pioneer Octave Chanute observed their experiments. He was impressed.

But Wilbur and Orville were far from satisfied. The lift was still not good enough and now there were problems with the controls.

Octave Chanute
Octave Chanute spent many years experimenting with flight before meeting the Wright brothers. He admired their work.

Lift
The air current beneath the wings gives an aircraft its lift.

Photography
Photography was a popular hobby of the time. Orville used this shed as a darkroom to develop photographs.

Camera
Early cameras took negatives of a picture on a metal plate instead of film.

Back in Dayton, Orville developed the latest photographs from Kitty Hawk. The pictures had recorded the glider experiments. When they analyzed data from their gliding experiments, they didn't make sense when compared to established data from Lilienthal and other flight pioneers.

"We've been relying on data collected by other people," said Orville, "but what if they're wrong?"

"We'll have to test all of the data ourselves," Wilbur replied.

Testing the data would prove a long task. They built a small wind tunnel. A fan at one end provided the wind.

Inside, the brothers placed miniature wings, or airfoils, mounted to test instruments so they could measure the lift and drag (the wings lifting or slowing down in the airflow). This was done to find the wing's curve, or camber. Although time-consuming, they both realized that the research was necessary.

Meanwhile, the Wrights were introduced to other experimenters. Octave Chanute had invited Wilbur to give an important lecture about human flight. For the occasion, Wilbur borrowed clothes from Orville's more stylish wardrobe. The speech was a great success.

Wind Tunnel
With the wind tunnel, the Wright brothers simulated flying conditions for their tests.

Always in Style
Orville was known for his fashionable clothes. He always liked to look smart, even when the work was dirty.

Wing Length
The brothers thought that the longer, narrower wings would improve lift.

DATE
1902

Using their new data, the Wright brothers designed a glider with longer, narrower wings and a different camber, or curve. They also redesigned the shape of the elevator at the front of the lower wing and added a fixed tail.

Rudder
A movable rudder turns the aircraft by directing the airflow on either side.

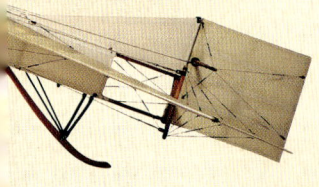

With high hopes, they went to Kitty Hawk. They immediately noticed the improved lift, but the fixed tail made control harder.

"Let's make the tail into a movable rudder to help with steering," suggested Orville.

Wilbur agreed. "We'll connect the rudder controls and the wing-warping controls so the pilot can work them together."

The brothers made the necessary changes and the plan worked. Wing-warping enabled the glider to roll by raising one wing and dipping the other. The elevator controlled pitch, moving the nose of the glider up or down. The movable rudder controlled yaw, turning the nose left or right. These three forms of control are still used in aircraft today.

Wilbur and Orville flew the improved glider again and again—sometimes 100 flights in one day at distances of more than 600 feet (182 m)! They had mastered the control and the lift of the aircraft. Now they turned their attention to adding power.

Roll
Roll allows the aircraft to bank, so that one wing is up, while the other is down.

Pitch
Pitch moves the nose up or down. For takeoff, the pitch needs to be up so the aircraft will rise.

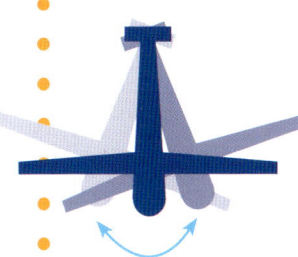

Yaw
Yaw turns the aircraft left or right, pointing it in the direction of the flight path.

Engine
The Wright brothers could not find a manufacturer to make a suitable engine, so they made one specially for the Flyer.

Aerodrome
Samuel Langley's pilot survived two crashes in his Aerodrome. The press made fun of Langley's attempts to fly, and Wilbur was wary of their reaction to his own trials.

THE WRIGHT FLYER

DATE
1903

With the help of Charlie Taylor, the mechanic at the bicycle shop, Wilbur and Orville built a small, lightweight engine. The Wright Flyer was the largest aircraft the Wrights had ever built. Orville called it a "whopper flying machine."

But at Kitty Hawk, parts kept breaking. Orville had to bring the propeller shafts, which held the propellers, back to Dayton for repair.

On the train back, he read newspaper reports about Samuel Langley's flying machine, which had crashed into a river near Washington, D.C.

On December 14, the Wright brothers were finally ready to attempt a flight.

The Kitty Hawk lifesaving crew arrived to help. The brothers flipped a coin to see who would be the pilot. Wilbur won.

The engine rumbled. Orville ran alongside to balance the wings, then the airplane flew off the launching rail and into the sky. The plane rose up sharply. Suddenly, it slowed, stalled, and the Wright Flyer sank into the sand.

The brothers were disappointed, but the flight had proved that the airplane could take off under the power of its own engine.

Lifesaving Crew
The job of the lifesaving crew was to rescue people from fishing boats. They enjoyed helping the Wright brothers with their flying experiments.

Winter Weather
When the Wright brothers awoke on the morning of December 17, 1903, and saw the bad weather, they discussed their options. They decided that despite the weather, they didn't want to wait any longer. They would try to fly again.

Bad weather meant the brothers had to wait to try again. On December 17, the wind was still gusting, but Wilbur and Orville were anxious to be home for Christmas, so they decided to have another attempt.

It was Orville's turn to fly. They set up the camera and asked John Daniels, a member of the lifesaving crew, to take a picture as the airplane took off. The two brothers shook hands, then Orville climbed into the pilot's position.

Everyone was solemn on what they hoped would be an historic day. "Don't look so serious," Wilbur urged. "Laugh and cheer and shout!"

The crew called encouragement as Orville took off. Quickly, Daniels snapped the photograph below as proof of the flight. The Flyer climbed and dived, up and down, several times, as Orville tried to steady the nose of the airplane.

He managed to stay in the air for 12 seconds. The plane landed on the sand about 120 feet (37 m) from where it had started. Wilbur and the crew cheered.

How Far Was the First Flight? The first controlled, powered flight was shorter than the main cabin of most commercial passenger planes.

National Memorial
A 60-foot
(18-m) granite
monument was
erected in 1932
to mark the site
of the Wright
brothers' flights
on December
17, 1903.

**Four Flight
Markers**
The distances
flown on the
four flights are
marked at the
site of the Wright
Brothers National
Memorial" as that
is the actual name.

The Wright brothers were delighted. Despite the strong wind, they took turns flying for a total of four flights.

During the fourth flight, the Flyer pitched up and down as Wilbur struggled to control the elevator—too far forward and the nose dived, too far back and it climbed too quickly. Finally it sank onto the sand. The flight had covered 852 feet (260 m) and lasted 59 seconds.

As Wilbur, Orville, and the lifesaving crew looked at the Flyer, a gust of wind rolled it over on the sand. Daniels tried to stop it, but when the Flyer finally came to rest, it had been reduced to a heap of broken wood and torn cloth. But the brothers had achieved their aim.

Johnny Moore, the youngest member of the lifesaving crew, was so excited, he raced to the village shouting, "They did it!"

Wilbur and Orville sat down to a quiet lunch. Then they sent a telegram home to their father and sister, telling them of the day's success, and adding that they would be home for Christmas.

Telegraph Machine
A telegram was the quickest way to send a message over long distances. The telegraph machine sent electrical signals over wires.

Form No. 168.
THE WESTERN UNION TELEGRAPH COMPANY.
INCORPORATED
23,000 OFFICES IN AMERICA. CABLE SERVICE TO ALL THE WORLD.

This Company TRANSMITS and DELIVERS messages only o. conditions limiting its liability, which have been assented to by the sender of the following message.
Errors can be guarded against only by repeating a message back to the sending station for comparison, and the Company will not hold itself liable for errors or delays in transmission or delivery of Unrepeated Messages, beyond the amount of tolls paid thereon, nor in any case where the claim is not presented in writing within sixty days after the message is filed with the Company for transmission.
This is an UNREPEATED MESSAGE, and is delivered by request of the sender, under the conditions named above.
ROBERT C. CLOWRY, President and General Manager.

170

RECEIVED at

176 C KA CS 33 Paid.   Via Norfolk Va

Kitty Hawk N C Dec 17

Bishop M Wright
            7 Hawthorne St

Success four flights thursday morning all against twenty one mile
wind started from Level with engine power alone average speed
through air thirty one miles longest 57 seconds inform Press
                                    Orevelle Wright   525P
home ~~past~~ Christmas .

Orville's telegram incorrectly recorded the longest flight as lasting 57 seconds, and misspelled his name.

Catapult Launcher

The catapult launcher had a pulley hanging from a tower. One end of the pulley held a weight. The other end was attached to a dolly holding the Flyer. When the weight dropped, the dolly zoomed forward, giving the Flyer enough speed for takeoff.

DATE 1904

Wilbur and Orville continued their experiments at a field near Dayton called Huffman Prairie. They built the Flyer II, a close copy of the original Flyer. In May, they invited reporters to watch a test flight. But the Flyer II hardly got off the ground. It needed more power to make up for the lack of wind in Dayton.

The brothers built a catapult launcher to boost speed during takeoff. They began to fly longer distances, and turn in the air. In September, Orville flew the first complete circle around Huffman Prairie.

But the Flyer II continued to have control problems. Then they added weight to the front of the plane to further improve control. The Flyer III worked.

On October 5, 1905, a small crowd watched as Wilbur flew around and around Huffman Prairie for a total of 24 miles (39 km). He landed after 39 minutes only because the engine had run out of fuel. It was by far the longest flight in history. The Wright brothers were now confident that they had invented a practical powered aircraft. In 1906 they received a patent for it.

Longest Flight
Wilbur's flight on October 5, 1905, was longer than all of the brothers' flights in 1903 and 1904 put together.

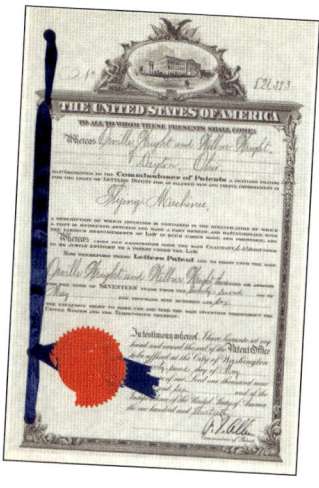

Legal Patent
A patent gives legal ownership of an invention. No one can use the idea without permission from the inventors.

Passengers
The first real airplane passenger was Charlie Furnas, the Wrights' mechanic.

Orville's Crash
Lt. Thomas Selfridge was the first person to be killed in an airplane. The brothers were very upset. When Orville found that a broken propeller blade caused the crash, they reinforced all of the blades to make flying as safe as possible.

FLYING FAR

Now Wilbur and Orville wanted to go into business selling their airplanes. But, they had trouble persuading people that their airplane was a practical flying machine. At last, the United States Army and a company in France both showed interest. At the Army's request, the brothers added space for a passenger, and included seats for both the pilot and the passenger. They built two airplanes.

In 1908, Wilbur sailed to France to demonstrate one of the planes, while Orville demonstrated the other near Washington, D.C. Both displays started quietly.

Then they both began staying in the air longer and longer, amazing the growing crowds below. News of the "birdmen" spread.

Newspapers pictured the brothers in competition. Wilbur and Orville took it all in fun.

"Your dandy flights make me look like a dud!" Wilbur joked in a letter from France.

Sadly, one of Orville's flights in September ended in tragedy with the death of his passenger, Lieutenant Thomas Selfridge.

Airplane Seats
Early airplane seats were open to the weather, and the pilots had to dress in warm clothes.

Birdman
This cartoon of Wilbur as a birdman was published in a French newspaper. His flights inspired many French aviators, who later broke Wilbur's own records.

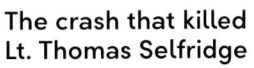

The crash that killed Lt. Thomas Selfridge

41

A Flight for a King?
The British king (above right) wanted to go on a flight with Wilbur, but his royal advisors wouldn't let him.

DATE 1909

Back in the United States, the Wright brothers were national heroes. They even received an award at the White House from President Taft, and they met the British king, Edward VII. In Dayton, there was a carnival and fireworks in their honor. Wilbur and Orville were embarrassed by the attention, but the rest of their family was full of pride.

The brothers set up the Wright Company to manufacture and sell airplanes. They also trained pilots to perform at exhibitions.

In October, nearly one million people gazed up at the sky in amazement as Wilbur flew over New York during the Hudson-Fulton celebrations. They cheered, tooting the horns of boats and cars. With so many witnesses to Wilbur's flight, many more people began to believe that humans could fly.

In 1910, the Wright brothers had one of their greatest thrills when Orville took their father for his first flight. Milton Wright was 81 years old.

"Higher, Orville!" he called. "Higher!"

Flips and Flops
Flips and Flops had two clowns that spun around a trapeze. One of the older Wright brothers opened a toy factory to manufacture it for sale to the public.

In 1912, Wilbur died of typhoid, the same disease that had nearly killed Orville so many years before.

Orville sold his share of the Wright Company a few years later. Sometimes, he still invented small things, such as a toy called Flips and Flops for his nieces and nephews. In 1948, he died quietly in Dayton.

Flyer III

Biplane

Airliner

Airliner
Airliners developed to carry people from place to place, on vacation or on business. By the 1950s, airliners were carrying about 100 passengers at a time.

With the invention of the airplane, Wilbur and Orville Wright made the dream of flight a reality. Flying makes travel easier and quicker, and as a result we know more about different people and places in all corners of the globe.

Military operations have altered dramatically through the development of aircraft.

The invention of the airplane has also led to technology that enables us to explore space, and that has led to communication satellites that allow telephones and computers to transmit signals around the world.

Supersonic Plane
Supersonic planes can fly faster than sound travels through the air. The Concorde was the first supersonic passenger plane.

The Concorde

BRITISH AIRWAYS

Space shuttle orbiter

When the young Wright brothers watched their toy helicopter fly into the air, they didn't know that in the years to come they would invent their own flying machine that would change the world.

Space Flight
The world's first reusable spacecraft, the space shuttle, blasted off with a throwaway fuel tank and two solid fuel rockets. It landed on a runway like a plane.

GLOSSARY

Airflow
The movement of air in a certain direction

Airfoil
A part of an aircraft, such as a wing, with curved surfaces that help to provide lift during flight

Biplane
An aircraft with two wings, one above the other

Camber
A curved surface, as in the curve of a wing

Data
Information, such as measurements, used in research

Drag
The air current that pushes back against an aircraft

Elevator
A flat surface that tilts to control the up and down movement of an aircraft's nose

Engine
A mechanical device that provides power

Fuel
A material, such as gasoline, that is burned for power

Glider
An aircraft with wings but no power. A glider must use natural airflow to stay aloft.

Helicopter
An aircraft with propellers on top that give it lift

Hot-air balloon
A balloon that rises because the hot air inside it is lighter than the cold air around it

Lift
The upward force of the airflow that enables an aircraft to takeoff and to stay in the air

Pioneer
A person, such as an inventor or explorer, who does something that hasn't been done before

Pitch
The up and down movement of an aircraft's nose

Propeller
Blades that push the air around, propelling an aircraft forward

Roll
Tilting one wing of the aircraft up and the other down

Thrust
A force that moves an aircraft forward

Wing-warping
A control mechanism on an aircraft in which the wings twist slightly, changing the airflow

Yaw
The movement of the aircraft to the left or right

INDEX

Aerodrome 32

airfoils 29

airliners 44

airplanes
  building/selling
    40–42
  first 32–35

bicycle clubs 14–15

bicycle repair shop 15–16

bicycles 14–17

biplane kite 20–21

biplanes 19, 20, 44

bird flight 19

birdman 41

Blériot, Louis 19

box twisting 20

camber 29, 30

cameras 28, 34

cars 16–17

catapult launcher 38

Cayley, Sir George 7

Chanute, Octave 27, 29

Concorde 45

cycling see bicycles

da Vinci, Leonardo 6

Daniels, John 34, 35, 36

drag 29

Edward VII, King 42

electric trains 24

elevator 22, 23, 30, 31, 36

engines 19, 32, 33

false teeth 12

first flights 32–37

Flips and Flops 44

Flyer 32–37

Flyer II 38–39

Flyer III 39, 44

flying experiments 22–31

flying machines 6–7

Furnas, Charlie 40

gas (gasoline) 17

gliders
  Cayley's 7
  Lilienthal's 7, 18
  Wright brothers'
    22–28, 30–31

helicopter, toy 8–9

horseless carriage 17

hot-air balloon 7

Hudson-Fulton
  celebrations 43

Huffman Prairie 38, 39

Icarus 6

kites 10, 20–21

Kitty Hawk 22–27, 30,
  32–33

Langley, Samuel 32

Leonardo da Vinci 6

lifesaving crew 33, 34,
  36–37

lift 19, 27, 29, 30

Lilienthal, Otto 7, 18

monoplanes 19

Montgolfier brothers 7

Moore, Johnny 37

National memorial 36

newspaper publishing 13

nose 31, 35, 36

ornithopter 6

passengers 40, 44

patent 39

photography 28

pilots 19, 22, 31

pitch 31

propellers 8, 32, 40

roll 31

rubber band 8, 9

rudder 30–31

Ruse, Cord 16–17

safety bicycles 14

St. Clair bicycle 16

Selfridge, Lt. Thomas 40,
  41

space shuttle orbiter 45

supersonic planes 45

tail 30

takeoff 31, 38

Tate, Bill 25

Tate, Tom 26

Taylor, Charlie 32

telegram 37

telegraph machine 37

toy helicopter 8–9

train systems 24

tuberculosis (TB) 12

typhoid 44

Van Cleve bicycle 16

Weather Bureau 22, 23

West Side News 13

wind tunnel 29

wing-warping 20, 31

wings
  biplane kite 20, 21
  bird 19, 20
  glider 22, 30, 31

woodcuts 10

Wright, Milton (father) 8,
  11, 37, 43

Wright, Orville, birth/
  death 8, 44

Wright, Susan (mother)
  11, 12

Wright, Wilbur, birth/
  death 8, 44

Wright Company 42, 44

Wright Cycle Company
  16

Wright Flyer see Flyer

yaw 31

QUIZ

Answer the questions to see what you have learned. Check your answers in the key below.

1. What toy inspired the brothers' interest in flying machines?

2. What was the brothers' first breakthrough in building a flying machine?

3. Where did the brothers test their first glider?

4. What did the brothers build to test data from their glider experiments?

5. What was the name of the largest aircraft that the brothers built?

6. What was the nickname that newspapers gave to the Wright brothers?

7. After the newspaper, what was the brothers' next business?

8. What are the three forms of control still used in aircraft today?

1. A toy helicopter 2. A biplane kite 3. Kitty Hawk, North Carolina, U.S.A. 4. A wind tunnel 5. Wright Flyer 6. "Birdmen" 7. A bicycle repair shop 8. Roll, pitch, and yaw

Dinosaur Detectives

Peter Chrisp

CONTENTS

6 Dinosaur Hunters

8 The Fossil Woman

16 The Strange Tooth

22 Dinner in a Dinosaur

26 The Bone Hunters

34 The Great Bone Rush

36 The Biggest Bone Dig

40 Dating the Dinosaurs

42 Baby Dinosaurs

46 Glossary

47 Index

48 Quiz

Mary Anning
Anning was one of the first fossil hunters. See page 8.

Gideon Mantell
This English doctor found a beast he called *Iguanodon*. See page 16.

Richard Owen
This English scientist held a party inside a concrete model of a dinosaur. See page 22.

DINOSAUR HUNTERS

Long, long ago, people all over the world began finding huge bones buried in sand or stone. Sometimes, these findings gave rise to stories about giants and dragons.

Today, we know these bones belonged to enormous beasts that lived millions of years ago. Some of them were land reptiles, called dinosaurs. Dinosaurs walked Earth for over 170 million years.

The dinosaurs died out, or became extinct, 66 million years ago.

In this book, you can read about some of the people who first discovered the truth about these huge bones. Like detectives, they worked to collect evidence and put together clues.

What they learned gives us a picture of life in the far distant past, when our world was the home of the dinosaurs.

Othniel Charles Marsh
This American and his rival Edward Cope hunted for fossils in the Old West. See page 34.

Werner Janensch
This German scientist went to Africa to dig for dinosaurs. See page 36.

Jack Horner
This American scientist dug up dozens of dinosaur nests. See page 42.

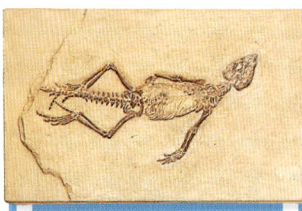

THE FOSSIL WOMAN

Welcome to my fossil shop! My name is Mary Anning. I've lived here in Lyme Regis, England, all my life. I was born in 1799 above this very shop, where my father was a carpenter.

For six days of the week, Father worked hard, making furniture. But on Sundays, he would take me for walks along the beaches to look for fossils. He sold them to the ladies and gentlemen who come to the seaside every summer.

Fossils Defined
Fossils are the remains of plants and animals, preserved in rock. Many fossils are bones that have gradually turned to stone.

Father taught me how to tap a rock in just the right place with a hammer to make it split open.

Often, there would be nothing inside it. But sometimes we would find the skeleton of a beautiful fish or a curly shell. We call the shells "snakestones" because they look like curled-up snakes. Scientists call them ammonites.

The best time to find fossils is after a storm, when the wind and waves batter and chip away at the cliffs. When a storm hits Lyme Regis, all sorts of strange creatures just fall out of the cliffs.

Father said that we were "fishing for curiosities." It was a bit like fishing because we never knew what we would catch. But our "fish" were made of stone.

Lyme Regis
This town on the south coast of England is still one of the best places in the world to find fossils.

Fossil Seller
Mary Anning (1799–1847) was the first person to make a living by selling fossils.

Ammonites
These ancient relatives of the squid lived in the sea and caught food with their tentacles.

Seashells
Anning's fossil discoveries made her famous. The tongue twister "she sells seashells on the sea shore" is thought by some to refer to her.

Fishing
Many people in Lyme Regis made their living from fishing in the sea.

My poor father died in 1810, when I was just 10 years old. Mother made some money by selling fish, but it was not enough for us to live on.

I knew that I had to work to help feed my family. I decided that I would spend all my time looking for curiosities to sell.

One day, I was looking for fossils with my brother, Joseph Anning. Walking along the beach, I looked at the cliff and saw something wonderful staring back at me.

It was the skull of a strange animal. And what a skull!

It must have been about 4 feet (1 m) long, with a big round eyehole and jaws stuffed with sharp teeth.

"It's a sea dragon, Mary!" said Joseph excitedly.

We hammered at the rocks until we could free the skull. Although it was very heavy, we managed to carry it home.

Joseph and I looked at pictures of animals in a book to see if we could discover what it was. We decided that it must be a crocodile.

Tools
Mary used simple tools, like this hammer and chisel, to split open rocks and chip out fossils.

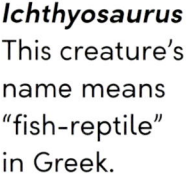

I was sure that the rest of the crocodile was still there, buried in the cliff. All I had to do was wait for another rockslide. So, after every storm, I would go back to the spot where we found the skull, hoping to see the rest of the skeleton.

It was almost a year later, in 1812, that the rocks finally fell away. There was my creature! But it wasn't a crocodile. Instead of legs, this animal had short paddles. It looked more like a fish!

I chipped the skeleton free with my hammer, and we carried it carefully back to our shop.

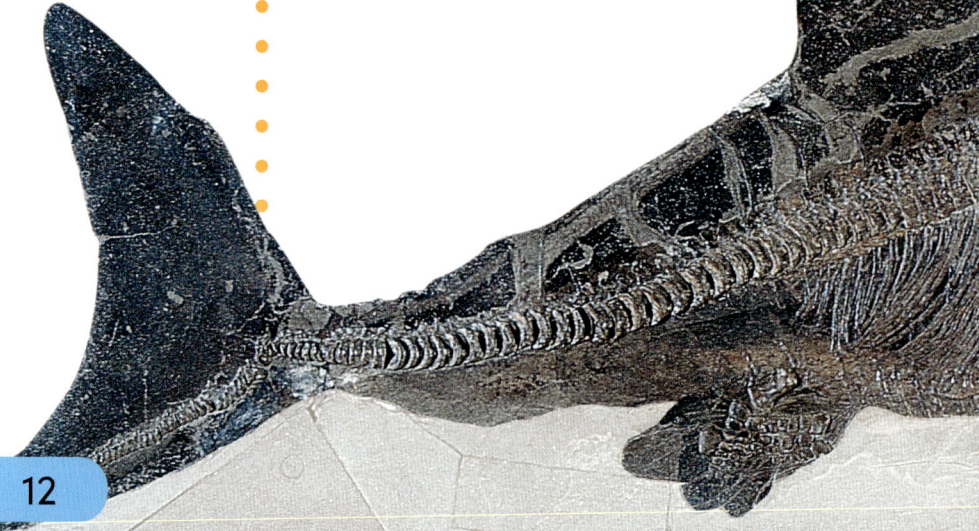

News quickly spread that the Annings had found a "sea dragon." Everyone wanted to have a look, and we were able to charge visitors some money to see it. Then, we sold the skeleton to a local nobleman for 23 pounds (about $29)—more money than I'd ever seen before.

At this time, I met my first geologists—scientific gentlemen who came to see the creature and argue about what it was. One of these geologists, Charles Konig, gave my creature a name: *Ichthyosaurus*.

Reptiles
This group of animals includes lizards and snakes. *Ichthyosaurus* was a reptile that swam like a fish.

Naming
Scientists give all plants and animals Greek or Latin names.

When I was 22 years old, I found an even stranger creature in the cliffs. It had a tiny head, an amazingly long neck, and four flippers.

It took me months to chip it free from the rocks, but it was time well spent. I was able to sell it to the Duke of Buckingham for 100 pounds (about $125).

I showed the skeleton to a geologist called William Conybeare, who visited me. His mouth dropped open in astonishment.

"I have never seen anything like this before!" he said. "It has the head of a turtle and the paddles of a whale. But its neck is like a giant snake. I shall call it *Plesiosaurus*, which means 'almost a reptile.'"

Plesiosaurus made me famous, although some geologists accused me of having created a fake fossil to make money.

Then, last year I discovered a reptile with wings! A fossil expert called William Buckland has named it *Pterodactylus macronyx*. He says that the poor beast must have drowned in the sea.

Of course, finds such as these are very rare. Mostly, I live by selling ammonites. Would you like to buy one?

Flying Reptiles
Anning's *Pterodactylus macronyx* was a pterosaur. Pterosaurs were flying reptiles that lived at the same time as the dinosaurs.

"Almost a Reptile"
William Conybeare published a description of the *Plesiosaurus* in 1821. He apologized for giving it such a "vague name."

Busy Doctor
Gideon Mantell (1790–1852) visited up to 60 patients a day. But he still found time to collect fossils and write a book called *The Geology of Sussex.*

Mary Ann Mantell
Mary Ann eventually lost patience with her husband's hobby. She left Gideon when his fossil collection took over their whole house!

THE STRANGE TOOTH

Ladies and gentlemen, thank you for coming to my lecture! My name is Gideon Mantell. Today, I am going to tell you about a remarkable discovery that I made in 1822.

At the time, I was a doctor in the English county of Sussex. Although I practiced medicine, my real interest was in geology. Between visits to patients, I would always find time to collect fossils.

One spring day, I was visiting a patient with my wife, Mary Ann Mantell. She had come with me to enjoy the fine weather. While I was busy, she strolled down the lane and saw a pile of rocks, used by workers to repair the roads.

In one of the rocks, Mary Ann noticed something brown and shiny. Looking closely, she saw that it was a very large tooth.

And here is that tooth! As you can see, it is worn away on the side from chewing, like the tooth of a plant-eating mammal. But it is an odd shape, with ridges. I had never seen anything like it.

The workers took me to the quarry, where I was amazed to learn that the tooth had come from a very old layer of rocks. No mammal fossil has ever been found in such rocks.

fossilized *Iguanodon* tooth

Teeth
Tooth shapes show what an animal eats. Plant eaters have short teeth for chopping and chewing leaves. Meat eaters have sharp, jagged teeth.

Rock Layers
Different types of fossils are found in different layers of rock. The oldest layers are the lowest in a rock face.

Buckland
William Buckland was the scientist who named Mary Anning's pterosaur.

Eccentric
Buckland kept a pet bear and often did chicken impressions in the middle of his lectures!

Clever Horse
Buckland's horse always stopped when she passed a quarry. She wouldn't move until he got off and looked for fossils.

I knew of one man who might be able to help me solve the mystery of the tooth. Only William Buckland has a bigger collection of fossils than I do. He has spent years collecting them from quarries around England.

I traveled to the professor's home in Oxford, England, and showed him the enormous tooth.

"Remarkable, sir!" said Buckland. "I fear I cannot help you to identify it. But let me show you a fossil!"

He led me to his desk, piled high with a jumble of rocks. Buckland pulled out a large bone and handed it to me.

I could see that it was a jaw, for it held a long, sharp, curved tooth. "It looks like a flesh eater," I said, "a very big flesh eater!"

"It was found in a slate quarry not far from here," said Buckland. "As you will observe, it is shaped like a lizard's jaw. Yet from the size of the tooth, this lizard must have been more than 40 feet (12 m)-long.

Think of that, sir—a 40-foot (12-m)-long flesh-eating lizard roaming around Oxfordshire!" I shuddered at the thought of it.

The professor went on, "I am going to call this great lizard a *Megalosaurus*."

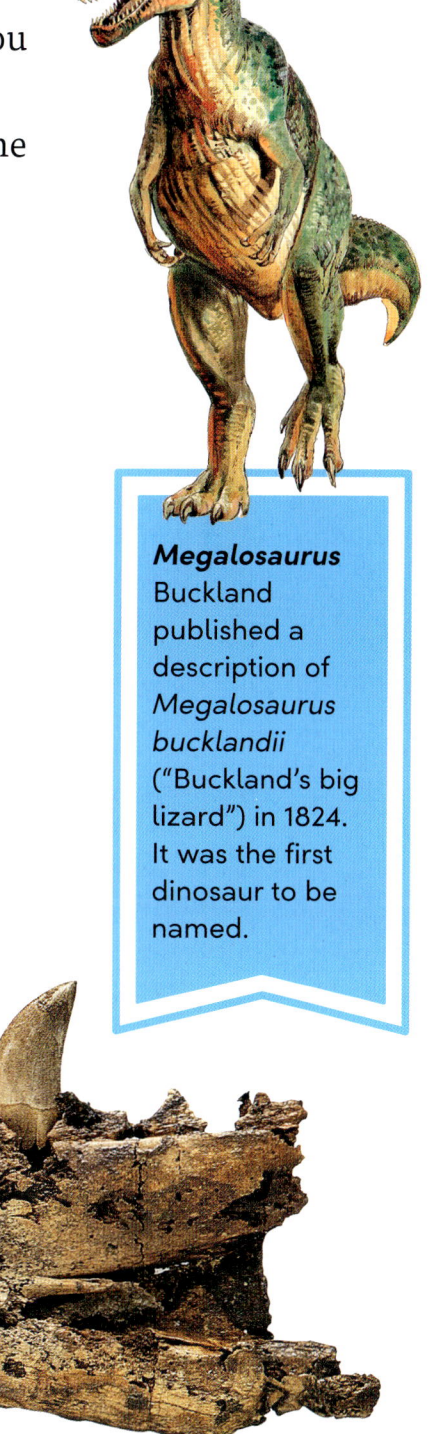

Megalosaurus
Buckland published a description of *Megalosaurus bucklandii* ("Buckland's big lizard") in 1824. It was the first dinosaur to be named.

jaw of *Megalosaurus*

Strange Meals
Buckland was famous for eating unusual animals. He always said that a mole was the most revolting thing he had ever tasted—until he ate a bluebottle fly.

Age of Reptiles
In 1838, Mantell published a book called *The Wonders of Geology*. It included this picture of a *Megalosaurus* attacking an *Iguanodon*.

Buckland invited me to stay for dinner, but I made excuses and left. I had heard that the professor ate odd things, like hedgehog meat.

As I traveled home, I thought about Buckland's discovery. I already knew of the giant sea reptiles discovered by Mary Anning at Lyme Regis. Now Buckland had found a huge land reptile.

Perhaps my tooth also came from an ancient reptile. Was it possible, I wondered, that before the time of the mammals, there had been an age of reptiles? I found my next clue in 1825 at the museum of the Royal College of Surgeons in London.

Looking through the collection of skeletons, I came across a South American lizard called an iguana. Its teeth were shaped just like the one I had found, with the same ridges. The only difference was that my tooth was 20 times bigger.

This convinced me that I had indeed found a reptile. I decided to call my reptile *Iguanodon*, or "iguana tooth."

Iguana
The South American iguana grows up to 5 feet (1.5 m) long. Mantell pictured his *Iguanodon* like an iguana, but 20 times bigger.

Iguanodon
Mantell published his description of *Iguanodon* in 1825. It was the second dinosaur to be named.

Skeleton Expert
Richard Owen was able to study many different skeletons by cutting up animals that died at the London Zoo.

Crowd Pleaser
In 1854, huge crowds went to the Crystal Palace in London to see the concrete models of *Iguanodon* and *Megalosaurus*.

Exhibition
Owen's models were the world's first dinosaur exhibition.

DINNER IN A DINOSAUR

I will never forget the party I went to in London on New Year's Eve in 1853. We ate our dinner inside an *Iguanodon*!

It was not a flesh-and-blood *Iguanodon*, of course. It was a brick and concrete model, built to show the public what these remarkable beasts might have looked like.

My name is Joseph Prestwick, and, like most of the guests on that evening, I'm a geologist.

At the head of our table sat our host, Richard Owen, an expert on animal skeletons. He had designed the splendid creature in which we sat.

Owen rose to his feet and said, "Fellow scientists! Let us drink to the memory of Gideon Mantell, discoverer of *Iguanodon*!"

We raised our glasses and cried, "Mantell!" There was a brief silence, as we each remembered the good doctor, who had died the previous year. It was sad indeed that Mantell was not there to see his discovery brought to life.

thumb

Nose Horn?
The concrete *Iguanodon* had a horn on its nose. Mantell and Owen had both misunderstood this bone. It was really the dinosaur's thumb!

As midnight approached, my friend Edward Forbes thanked our host for the splendid meal.

Forbes said, "We owe Owen a great deal, gentlemen. Gideon Mantell and William Buckland thought of their discoveries as overgrown lizards. But in the 1830s, more bones of these huge reptiles were found, and Owen studied them closely.

"Owen has a great understanding of skeletons. He could see that, unlike lizards, these creatures held their bodies off the ground on straight legs. They were not giant lizards. They were a separate group of animals, which Owen has named *Dinosauria*.

Standing Tall
Straight legs are better at bearing weight than the sprawling legs of lizards. It was thanks to their straight legs that dinosaurs could grow so much bigger than any other reptiles.

And now, if I may," Forbes added, "I would like to read you a poem that I have written. It is about this magnificent *Iguanodon* in which we are sitting.

A thousand ages underground
His skeleton had lain;
But now his body's big
 and round
And he's himself again!
The jolly old beast
Is not deceased,
There's life in him again!"

At this, we all let out a huge roar like a bellowing herd of *Iguanodon*.

Dinosauria

Two Legs or Four?
Owen mistakenly believed that all dinosaurs walked on four legs. Later finds showed that many walked on their hind legs, like this *Giganotosaurus*.

Dinosaurs
In 1841, Owen invented the name "dinosaur." It means "terrible lizard" in Greek.

Expeditions
In the 1870s, Othniel Charles Marsh (1831–1899) led his students on four fossil-hunting expeditions to the West.

Railroad
In the 1860s, the Union Pacific Railroad was built across the USA to link the cities of the East with the West.

THE BONE HUNTERS

My name is Matthew Randall, but all my friends call me Matty. Let me tell you about my young days out in the American West.

Back in 1868, I found work on the building of the Union Pacific Railroad. Laying those iron rails was hard work, and it was dangerous, too. This was the homeland of the Sioux, who hated the railroad.

For months on end, we lived on fried bison steaks, provided by our own hunter, "Buffalo Bill" Cody.

One day, a group of strangers rode into our camp. There were about a dozen youngsters led by an older fellow.

"Good day," said the older man. "I am Othniel Charles Marsh of Yale University, and these are my students. We are on a bone-hunting expedition!"

This struck me as an odd occupation, although I was too polite to say so.

Buffalo Bill
William Cody earned his nickname by supplying the railway workers with bison meat. He was famous for his skill as a scout.

Sioux
The Sioux depended on bison for food, clothes, tools, and tents. The settlers and the railroad ruined Sioux hunting grounds.

Museum
Marsh was the nephew of George Peabody, a millionaire banker. He used his uncle's money to build the Peabody Museum at Yale University to house his fossils.

Darwin
In 1859, naturalist Charles Darwin suggested that animals are not fixed in one permanent form, or species. They change over time, to produce new species. He called this "evolution."

Marsh had come to our camp to meet up with Buffalo Bill, who had offered to be his guide on the bone-hunting expedition.

Next morning, the bone hunters rode off. Buffalo Bill led the way and Marsh rode beside him. They had an escort of cavalrymen and six wagons. We wished them well and then went back to our work on the railroad.

More than a month later, we met up with Marsh again. His students now looked like real westerners, with tanned faces and well-worn clothing.

Marsh was full of stories of his adventures. He said that he'd shot an angry bull bison that was charging at him. He'd also made friends with some Sioux, who called him "Big Bone Chief."

Then, he showed us the wagonloads of bones he'd collected. He handed one of them around.

"Here's a real treasure," he said. "It's a bird's skull with teeth in its beak! This shows that birds must have evolved from reptiles. It proves that Charles Darwin was right about evolution!"

We had no idea what he was talking about.

Bird with Teeth
Darwin's followers believed that one group of dinosaurs grew feathers and took to the air. They evolved into birds. Early birds kept some reptile features, such as teeth.

Proof
Darwin's supporters hoped to find fossils that would prove his theory. This was why Marsh was excited to find a bird's skull with teeth.

Headdress
Sioux warriors wore eagle feather headdresses.

Black Hills
The Sioux fought for the Black Hills. They won a victory at the Battle of the Little Bighorn in 1877, but eventually they lost their territory.

Marsh said that if we ever found any unusual bones, we should write to him at Yale. Then, he went home with his students and his collection of bones. I guessed that this was the last I would hear of bone hunting.

Over the next years, big changes came to the West. The railroads I helped to build brought thousands of settlers from the East. New towns sprang up all over the place.

In 1874, gold was discovered in the Black Hills in Sioux territory. Soon, we had a real gold rush, with trainloads of easterners arriving, all hoping to strike it rich. The Sioux fought to defend their land, but they were forced to move to reservations.

I'd found a job looking after the train depot at a little place called Como Bluff in Wyoming, USA. I had plenty of free time and I'd often walk up into the hills.

There wasn't much to look at there—just a lot of dry, bare rocks.

But one day in 1877, I found a bone sticking out of the rocks that was bigger than I was! Nearby, there was another huge bone, and another. These bones seemed to go on for miles.

Teepees
Before they were forced to stay on reservations, the Sioux made good use of portable homes called teepees. These were made of bison hide stretched over wooden poles.

Bare Rocks
The rocky hills of Wyoming, USA, have been worn away by rivers, rain, and wind. These areas, called badlands, are wonderful places to find fossils.

Cope
Edward Drinker Cope (1840–1897) wrote more than 1,400 books and articles and named more than 1,000 new animal species.

Spies
Both Marsh and Cope hired spies to keep an eye on what the other one was doing. They also used bribes to win over diggers from the rival team.

I was going to send a letter to Marsh, but then I heard that a rich bone-hunting professor had arrived in Canon City, not far away.

I traveled there, expecting to find Marsh. But I was surprised to see a different fellow. He said his name was Edward Drinker Cope.

I asked him if he knew Marsh. "Marsh!" shouted Cope, turning red in the face. "The man is a fraud and a thief!" It seemed that Cope hated Marsh worse than poison.

When I told him about the bones I had found, he offered me $100. I had to show him the place and keep it a secret from Marsh's spies.

Cope soon had a team of diggers at work, blasting the rock with gunpowder and prying the bones out with crowbars. Many bones shattered and were thrown away.

But Cope couldn't keep his secret forever. One day, a team of Marsh's diggers showed up. It was just like the days of the gold rush, only these fellows were after bones.

Broken Bones
Eventually, the diggers invented ways to protect the bones they dug up. Marsh's men wrapped them in strips of cloth, soaked in flour and water. Cope's men used boiled rice instead of flour.

Useful Technique
The practice of wrapping fossils in cloth and plaster of Paris is still used on some digs today.

Feud
Cope and Marsh fell out when Marsh pointed out that Cope had reconstructed a sea reptile with its head on the end of its tail. This humiliated Cope, who never forgave Marsh.

Heavy Reptile
Barosaurus belonged to the sauropod family of dinosaurs, which were the largest animals ever to walk Earth.

THE GREAT BONE RUSH

Cope and Marsh each had teams of diggers working all over the West. It was a race to describe and name all the new species. As a result of this "bone rush," they discovered almost 130 new kinds of dinosaur.

Cope worked alone, but Marsh had a team of expert assistants to help him put the skeletons together.

Marsh's dinosaurs came in many shapes and sizes. There was the flesh-eating *Allosaurus* ("different reptile") and gigantic plant eaters like the *Barosaurus* ("heavy reptile").

Triceratops

There were also dinosaurs with horns, such as the *Triceratops* ("three-horned face").

The strangest dinosaur of all was one Marsh called *Stegosaurus* ("roofed reptile"). It had rows of mysterious bony plates all along its back.

Meanwhile, Cope and Marsh attacked each other in newspaper articles. Their squabbling made both of them look silly, but it also made "dinosaur" a household word.

Roofed Reptile
Scientists still argue about what the *Stegosaurus* used its plates for. Some think they helped the animal control its temperature. Others believe they were used to signal to other dinosaurs.

Allosaurus

Stegosaurus

Life's Work
Werner Janensch (1878–1969) spent the rest of his life working on the bones he brought back from Africa.

Leg Bone
Brachiosaurus was so big that its femur (upper leg bone) was as long as a person!

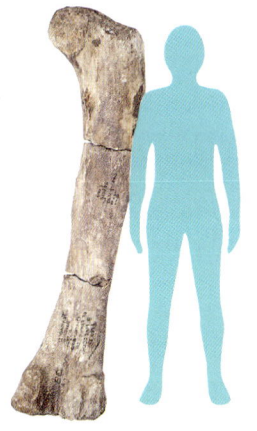

THE BIGGEST BONE DIG

My name is Werner Janensch. I've just come home to Germany after spending three years in Africa, leading a huge dig.

Back in 1907, I heard that some giant bones had been found at a place called Tendaguru in East Africa. I raised the money for an expedition and sailed to Africa in 1909.

I hired hundreds of local people to help me with the project. Tendaguru lies far inland, and there are no roads. All our food and supplies had to be carried on foot from the coast. The bones we dug up had to be carried back in the same way.

I was expecting to find new dinosaurs in Africa.

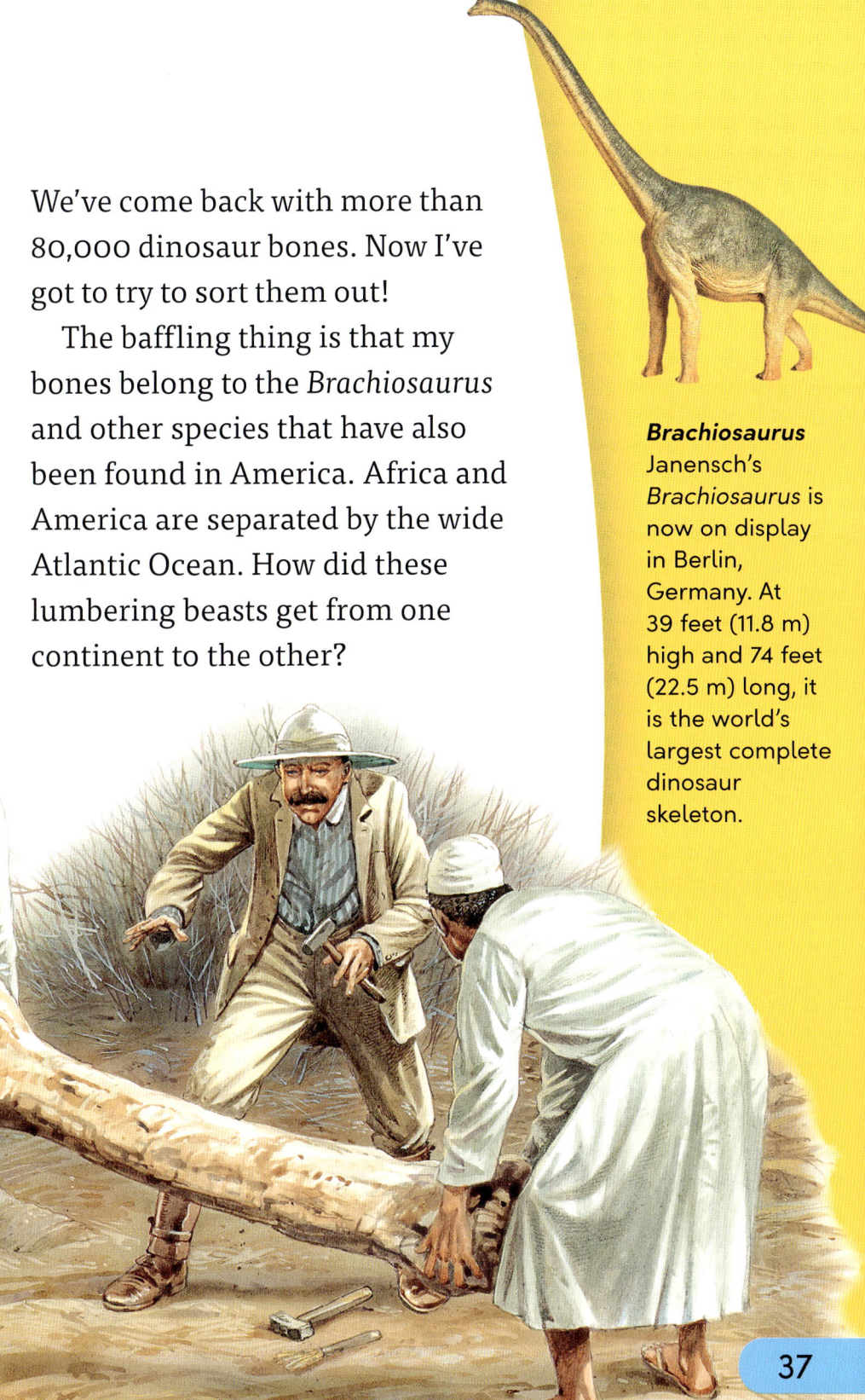

We've come back with more than 80,000 dinosaur bones. Now I've got to try to sort them out!

The baffling thing is that my bones belong to the *Brachiosaurus* and other species that have also been found in America. Africa and America are separated by the wide Atlantic Ocean. How did these lumbering beasts get from one continent to the other?

Brachiosaurus
Janensch's *Brachiosaurus* is now on display in Berlin, Germany. At 39 feet (11.8 m) high and 74 feet (22.5 m) long, it is the world's largest complete dinosaur skeleton.

Wegener
In 1912, Alfred Wegener suggested that there was once only one huge landmass, which he called "Pangaea." He believed that it had split into pieces. The pieces slowly drifted apart to form the continents that we know today.

Wild Theory
At the time, few scientists took Wegener's theory of "continental drift" seriously. It was not until the 1960s that he was proved right.

In Berlin, Germany, I showed my *Brachiosaurus* skull to some of our geologists. "This is an American dinosaur," I explained. "How did it end up in Africa? It's a mystery!"

Most of them were puzzled. But a young man called Alfred Wegener said, "It's not a mystery at all. This is exactly the type of dinosaur I would expect to find in Africa!"

Wegener pulled out a world map. "Look at the coastlines of Africa and South America. Their shapes match exactly. I believe that they must have once been joined.

Somehow, they have drifted to their present positions.

"This is why you found the same dinosaurs in Africa and America. When your *Brachiosaurus* was alive, there was no Atlantic Ocean!"

We were all startled by this wild theory. "Are you seriously suggesting that continents can roam around Earth's surface?" I asked. "How is this possible?"

"I don't know," said Wegener. "But your *Brachiosaurus* is the proof that I am right!"

Drifting Continents
We now know that Earth's surface is made up of several enormous plates floating on top of molten rock. Forces inside Earth move the plates slowly. This is what made the continents move and split apart.

270 million years ago

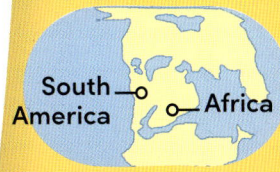

130 million years ago

Present day

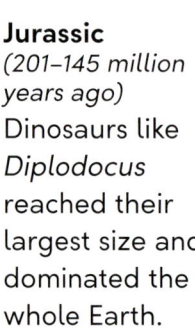

DATING THE DINOSAURS

Like detectives, early geologists collected evidence to piece together the story of life on Earth. Using fossils, they were able to place different periods of Earth's history in order. They gave these periods names based on the type of rocks in which the various fossils were found.

The age of the dinosaurs was divided into three periods: Triassic, when dinosaurs first evolved; Jurassic, when they became the main land animals; and Cretaceous, when new sorts, such as the horned dinosaurs, appeared.

Geologists knew that Triassic dinosaurs must have lived before Jurassic ones. But they could only guess how long ago that was.

It was not until the 1920s that scientists were able to work out the age of rocks. This was thanks to the study of radioactivity.

Many rocks are made up of elements that are radioactive. These elements slowly decay, or break down, to form other elements. Scientists measure the amount of a radioactive element in a rock. They can then work out how long the decay has been going on and so when the rock was formed.

Radioactive decay is like a clock, ticking away inside Earth's rocks. Using this clock, scientists were able to date the rocks that held the dinosaur fossils.

This told them when the dinosaurs had lived.

Cretaceous
(145–66 million years ago)
This was the age of the horned dinosaurs, such as this *Protoceratops*.

Elements
Elements are the basic substances, such as carbon, potassium, and uranium, that all things are made of.

Jack Horner
Jack Horner (1946–) is one of the world's leading experts on dinosaurs. He was the technical adviser for the films *Jurassic Park* and *The Lost World*.

Paleontology
A modern dinosaur detective is called a paleontologist. Paleontology is the study of ancient life. It comes from the Greek word *palaios*, which means "ancient."

BABY DINOSAURS

In 1978, a paleontologist named Jack Horner was visiting a fossil shop in Montana, USA. He found the bones of a baby dinosaur. This was an important discovery. Few baby dinosaurs had ever been found!

Horner traced the fossil back to the rocky hillside where it had been discovered and began to dig. Soon, he had uncovered a huge nest. It was over 6 feet (2 m) wide and contained 15 baby dinosaurs and lots of crushed eggshells.

In the 1980s, Horner's team found more nests at the site. Some of them contained eggs and newly hatched babies.

Horner knew that the soil around the nests could hold clues.

By sifting the soil and examining it under a microscope, he discovered the remains of chewed-up leaves and berries. He also found dinosaur droppings, containing woody debris from conifer trees. Can you work out what he discovered?

Horner used these clues and other evidence to build an amazing picture of the lives of these dinosaurs.

Fossilized Baby
Horner's team chipped away the rock to discover this fossilized eggshell containing a baby hatchling.

Herds
Fossil footprints are further evidence that some dinosaurs, such as these *Gallimimus*, traveled in herds. The young stayed in the middle of a herd, while the adults walked on either side to provide protection.

Horner's most important discovery was that the babies were being looked after by their parents. He called this dinosaur *Maiasaura*, which means "good mother lizard."

The evidence for parental care was the size of the 15 babies. Since they were three times bigger than newly hatched ones, they must have stayed in their nest for weeks after hatching. They had crushed the eggshells in their nest as they moved around. The chewed-up leaves and berries were food brought by the parents.

The mystery is why the babies died. Perhaps something happened to their parents, and the babies starved to death in the nest.

In 1984, Horner's team made another discovery. They found the bones of 10,000 *Maiasaura* that had been killed by a volcanic eruption. Finding so many animals together shows that they lived in huge herds.

Like Modern Animals
Horner says, "Dinosaurs basically aren't any different from animals alive today. They just looked different."

Nest Site
Horner thinks that these *Maiasaura* returned to the same nest site year after year, just like many birds and turtles do today.

GLOSSARY

Ammonite
A prehistoric sea creature with a coiled shell

Continental drift
The theory that the continents were once joined together, split apart, and drifted to their present positions

Cretaceous
The third period in the age of dinosaurs, 145 to 66 million years ago

Dinosaurs
Land reptiles that lived on Earth for over 170 million years and died out 66 million years ago

Elements
The basic substances, such as hydrogen, carbon, and iron, that all things are made of

Evolution
The theory that species of animals and plants gradually change over long periods of time to produce new species

Extinct
No longer existing

Fossils
Traces of animals and plants, preserved in rocks, including bones, skin, and footprints

Geology
The study of Earth and its rocks

Jurassic
The second period in the age of dinosaurs, 201 to 145 million years ago

Mammals
A group of warm-blooded animals with hair. Mammals give birth to live young, which feed on milk.

Naturalist
A scientist who studies animals and plants

Paleontology
The study of ancient life, from the Greek word *palaios*, which means "ancient"

Pterosaurs
Flying reptiles that lived at the same time as the dinosaurs

Quarry
A place where stone is dug out of the ground

Radioactivity
The energy released by elements, such as uranium, as they break down, or decay. Radioactivity can be used to date rocks.

Reptiles
A group of cold-blooded, egg-laying animals with scaly skins

Sauropods
A group of huge, long-necked dinosaurs

Species
A group of animals or plants that can breed together and that share few differences

Triassic
The first period in the age of dinosaurs, 252 to 201 million years ago